Foreword

Students of the educational scene today often note the existence of strong national concern for improving the quality of education and a renewal of the historic American commitment to equalizing educational opportunities for all children and youth. Improved preparation of school personnel is a parallel, though less obvious, concern. These concerns have provided the stimulus for more rapid and more substantial improvements in education in recent years than have been achieved in any previous generation.

As might be expected, programs of preparation for professional careers in education are currently the subject of careful study, inasmuch as improving education is partially a function of improved personnel. One of the most important ways of viewing programs for preparing professional educators is two-dimensional, basic or foundational preparation and specialized preparation. The former can be conveniently defined, although perhaps the definition is an oversimplification, as being made up of content appropriate to all professional educators while the latter is that preparation which is designed to prepare a person for a particular responsibility in the profession, for example, a first-grade teacher, or a high school biology teacher, or a school superintendent. Neither dimension of preparation is adequate alone. The foundations area provides needed professional perspective, knowledge of the cultural orientation of schools, philosophical directions of education, knowledge of human growth and development, learning theory, the primary methodology of teaching, and evaluation of learning outcomes. Specialization is preparation for discharging the responsibilities inherent in the particular position one holds in the educational system.

As is true of preparation programs for other major professions, those for professional educators make use of content from several disciplines. Such content is organized according to the purposes to be served by the particular program and requires adaptations to these purposes. As implied above, preparation for careers in education relies on the disciplines of philosophy, educational psychology, sociology, anthropology, and others for its content, as well as on the discipline of education. The subject matter selected from these supporting disciplines and applied to teacher education makes up the area of professional preparation known as the Foundations of Education. Such subject matter must take form in a meaningful pattern with interrelationships of the content from the respective disciplines made clear. When this occurs, a set of useful generalizations about education, its goals, its setting, its characteristics, effective teaching and the proper evaluation of learning is possible. These generalizations are critical in the development of a professional educator and without them only educational technicians are possible.

The *Foundations of Education Series* edited by Dr. Ray C. Phillips and Dr. Robert J. Stalcup properly emphasizes this important dimension of teacher education. There is a definite and important place in professional literature for this series. It should add much to the further professionalization of preparation for careers in education.

Truman M. Pierce, Dean
School of Education
Auburn University
Auburn, Alabama

Preface

This publication, like the others in this series, is designed to give the student of professional education an overview of a specific area within the professional education field.

Keeping up with the tremendous amount of writing published each year in the field of education poses, in itself, a virtually impossible task. For this reason the authors have felt a strong need to provide students with a capsule presentation of some of the basic concepts included in the major areas of study in professional education.

The use of this series of works should serve to give the student direction in carrying on more extensive study in those areas in which he is weak. The selective bibliography included in each of these publications should provide a point of departure for any additional investigation which the student feels is necessary. In any event the authors take the position that these publications represent the minimum information which any student of education needs to have.

R. C. Phillips
R. J. Stalcup
Editors

Methodology in Education

Richard K. Means

School of Education
Auburn University

Foundations of Education
Series

Charles E. Merrill Publishing Company, Columbus, Ohio
A Bell & Howell Company

Merrill's Foundations of Education Series under the editorship of Dr. Ray C. Phillips, Auburn University, and Dr. Robert J. Stalcup, The Education Commission of the States.

Library of Congress Catalog Card Number: 68-14079

2 3 4 5 6 7 8 9 10—76 75 74 73 72 71 70

PRINTED IN THE UNITED STATES OF AMERICA

71 2009 435

Table of Contents

Chapter 1

Introduction and Orientation

Nothing in education is so astonishing as the amount of ignorance it accumulates in the form of inert facts.

Henry Adams

Introduction

Present-day education is ultimately dedicated to the optimal growth and development of each individual. It is intimately concerned with the physical, intellectual, mental, social, emotional, and spiritual behavior of the learner. The activities and experiences that assist in the realization of educational objectives are the aims and the methods of instruction.

Teachers and other directors of learning are necessarily aware of those conditions that enhance or interfere with most effective educational progress. Among the most aggravating and persistent instructional problems are those closely associated with method. Frequently teachers seek answers to such questions as: How can I stimulate my students to really learn? What concepts create the greatest learning difficulty? Which lessons seem to be most dull, unchallenging, and least retained by students? These are questions which can be answered only by the teacher. The essential ingredients for dealing with them, however, lie in a basic understanding of accepted principles of learning, motivation, behavioral characteristics, and the techniques and methods of teaching.

1

This does not suggest that the teacher should be the dominant factor in the classroom for modern research indicates the importance of learning involvement.

Brief Historical Background

Certain methods, procedures, and techniques of instruction obviously have been utilized throughout the long evolution of education. These approaches generally have coincided with the existing philosophies of education and the predominant theories of learning in vogue during any given period. There is ample evidence to suggest that many "modern" methods of teaching are, in fact, adaptations of instructional procedures that were probably used in the past.

Many teaching methods and techniques have been used for many generations with relatively little alteration. Certain of these approaches, time-tested during the evolution of educational practice, still occupy a prominent and rightful place in the scheme of instruction at all levels. Some of the major historical influences and important personalities who contributed to educational methodology include:

Ancient Greece. The Greeks sought excellence in philosophical thought and emphasized education as a social institution. Many methods utilized in teaching would be considered "progressive" today, such as group discussion, field trips and excursions, games and sports, forums, debate and argumentation, rhythmic activities, and learning through participation.

Socrates, whose guiding principle was "know thyself," emphasized dialectic (question and answer), discussion, inquiry, dialogue, and conversation. "Teaching," he said, "is the direction of activities." The Socratic Method consisted of a five step proposition with reference to an idea—question, analyze, reason, conclusion, and generalization.

The idealist Plato organized a more authoritative approach concerning the science of ideas which included among other things the use of dialectic and intuitive reasoning. Aristotle advocated learning by direct experience. "Education," he perceived, "is a lifelong activity and a function of the state." He recommended the inductive method with objective experimentation, scientific observation, and rational thought and conduct.

Ancient Rome. The curriculum of the Romans was designed to provide a general education with an emphasis on logic, rhetoric, oratory, debate, and legal training. They sought a kind of practical ability involving a knowledge of the law. Cicero viewed rhetorical style as important and professed that "the educated man is an orator."

The aim of education, according to the great teacher Quintilian, was to produce a virtuous, learned, and fluent man. He stressed a progressive methodology which entailed motivation through interest, leading rather than driving, and making studies pleasant. Plutarch strongly believed in training of the mind and body through useful habits. In his classic *On the Education of Children,* he recognized the modification of methods to individual differences.

The Middle Ages. Education in the Middle Ages sought to preserve the educational thought and practice of the Greco-Roman period. Although education was almost exclusively religious in nature, rudiments of earlier teaching methods were maintained in programs of the church and monasteries.

Alcuin utilized a process of instruction, prominent in catechetical schools, which reflected predominantly the question and answer procedure. Monastic schools served to perpetuate classical education and were devoted to the lore and laws of the church, music, vocational arts, and physical fitness. The convent schools of the era were concerned with such subjects and activities as rhetoric, Latin, weaving, needlework, and music.

The Renaissance. More practical education for the complete citizen—physically, mentally, socially, and morally—marked the Renaissance period. Instructional materials were reorganized and general methodology changed. Educational organization into elementary, secondary, and higher schools also evolved. Apprenticeship or Guild Schools likewise provided vocational education innovations. The father of secondary education, Vittorino De Feltre, placed great attention on individual differences and practical education, seeking the all-round development of student personality—health, sociability, citizenship, aesthetic enjoyment, and ethical character. "We are all responsible," he asserted of teachers, "for the personal influence which goes forth from us." His Italian counterpart, Guarino Da Verona, founded court schools which stressed improved teaching methods. He particularly used a seminar-type teaching which emphasized physical, mental, and moral development.

Sixteenth and Seventeenth Centuries. The 1500's and 1600's were characterized by expanded curricula and a new concern for science and the practical arts. Education emphasized piety, knowledge, and various forms of expression. Increased travel opportunities and the development of printing aided the spread of new educational theories and methods of instruction. The value of imitation as a part of the learning process was identified by Roger Ascham, tutor to Queen Elizabeth I. Michel de Montaigne advocated conversation, reading, and demonstration. Francis Bacon refined and popularized the inductive method of instruction, rejected formal verbal learning, and stressed the spirit of free inquiry through experimentation and observation.

The educational reformer and progenitor of modern education, Johann Amos Comenius, provided one of the first scientific approaches to education with his high regard for sense perception and science. "Teaching," he proposed, "should be true, full, clear, and solid." John Locke, the founder of modern psychology and author of *Conduct of the Human Understanding,* stressed the importance of habit and discipline in the faculty or "tabula rasa" theory of learning.

Modern Foreign Developments.   The application of earlier theories and the development of new practices brought gradual change to educational methodology and education in general after 1700. New fields of study, such as architecture, nature, physiology, and bookkeeping, brought forth innovations in instructional procedure. The work of a number of prominent educators also influenced modern-day thought and action.

Jean Jacques Rousseau promoted the naturalist view of education through sensual perception, moral training by example, habit formation, and direct experience. "Education," he suggested, "should follow the natural order of the child's development." The father of elementary education, Johann Heinrich Pestalozzi, stressed the use of the immediate environment for learning through observation, sense impression, and investigation. He viewed education as "a natural, symmetrical, and harmonious development of the whole child." A new psychology of learning was introduced by Johann Friedrich Herbart. He identified five formal steps of instruction—preparation, presentation, comparison and abstraction, generalization, and application. Friedrich Froebel, the originator of the kindergarten, recognized the educational value of play, games, motor expression, songs, language symbols, self-activity, and participation in the natural environment. Herbert Spencer, author of the classic *Education: Intellectual, Physical and Moral,* favored instruction which was pleasurable and interesting; learning that proceeded from the simple to the complex, and the scientific laboratory method.

Developments in the United States. The value of early education in the colonies was determined by its relation to the religious and vocational needs of the times. Reflections of the various educational philosophies of naturalism, idealism, realism, and humanism were evidenced in later periods, along with new innovations and applications. Curriculum changes as well as alterations in methodology occurred with the implementation of mass education in the United States.

Benjamin Franklin strongly promoted education as a life process and was noted for his early book *Proposals Relating to the Education of Youth.* He suggested that instructional methods should be such as to lead to scientific experimentation, observation, and application. Samuel R. Hall started the first teacher training institution in the nation and wrote the first professional book in English, *Lectures on Schoolkeeping,* which dealt in part with methods of instruction.

One of the founders of the American public school system was Horace Mann. His broad concept of education and school organizational genius did much to influence methodology in the field. Edward A. Sheldon was responsible for the introduction of Pestalozzian methods and ideas in the United States. His approach to instruction emphasized sense perception, reason, and judgment. Thomas Jefferson, Henry Barnard, William T. Harris, and Charles W. Eliot were other early leaders who contributed to American education.

John Dewey stressed education as life and viewed the school as a miniature society. "The best educational method," he proposed, "is the reconstruction of experience." He emphasized learning by doing through the scientific method and through problem solving. Originality, interest, and initiative were important elements of the process. His means of education favored play, use of tools, construction, contact with nature, expression, and purposeful activity.

The United States, although noted for numerous innovations in educational organization and methodology, strongly borrowed ideas and practices from other countries. The most casual visitor to a modern school cannot help but be impressed by the general variety and scope of teaching approaches. The perspective gained by understanding the evolution of methodology in education should be helpful in developing an appreciation of the instructional methods, procedures, and techniques which are discussed on the following pages.

The Art of Teaching

There is obviously much more to good teaching than learning to construct attractive visual materials, run complicated instructional equipment, or organize and conduct group activities. Effective teaching requires a deep understanding of human nature, individual behavior, group interaction, and the phenomenon of learning itself.

Values of Meaningful Experience. Freehill emphasized the importance of meaningful experience in relation to good teaching:

> Quality teaching is purposeful. It moves toward the development of a mature people and recognizes the student as an insightful participant in his own learning. It formulates convictions, and it fosters willingness to act by these convictions. Without such learning, man would stand eternally hungry in the wet cold of the cave in which he began.[1]

It is becoming increasingly apparent that concepts and ideas are more easily and firmly grasped when presented in more than a single way. Instruction which supplements teacher verbalization with something projected on a screen, drawn on the chalkboard,

---

[1] Maurice F. Freehill, "How We Learn," *NEA Journal,* 47: 324-27, May, 1958, p. 327.

resolved through group deliberation, or played on a recording machine, is often infinitely more effective. It also is evident that each technique and procedure of instruction has its own peculiar and characteristic nature as well as its own unique, fundamental advantages and limitations. The effective use of different teaching methods requires skill in planning, selecting, preparing, adapting, utilizing, and appraising. It likewise involves a functional understanding of the "why" as well as the "what" and the "how."

Basic Classroom Considerations. Certain classroom factors or considerations have been identified which help in the stimulation of learning. Some of these were succinctly presented by Sartor. She posed the following questions, all with strong application to method:

Do I make my assignments clear and specific so that each pupil knows what is expected of him?

Do I provide for individual differences in the classroom?

Do I *encourage* my pupils to work rather than *drive* them?

Do I teach with all the knowledge at my command, yet avoid acting like a know-it-all?

Do I try to relate subject-matter to actual life experiences?

Do I recognize the worth of each individual and encourage creativeness rather than expect students to conform to a pattern?

Am I able to communicate with my pupils in all areas of their interests?

Do I make good use of all available teaching materials and watch for new materials as they are developed?

Do I use frequent evaluations to check pupil accomplishment?[2]

It clearly is evident that teachers guide students by the words that they utter, the things that they do, the way that they act, and by the skillful manipulation of the environment. They influence behavior by providing activities that stimulate student thinking, feeling, and action. They plan experiences that give encourage-

---

[2] Lina Sartor, "How Good a Teacher Am I?" *NEA Journal*, 45: 448, Oct., 1956.

ment to creativity, enriched interests, and originality of expression. They help students to analyze situations, identify their problems, plan and evaluate their progress, and establish worthwhile goals.

The Learning Process

Much has been written concerning the complex phenomenon of learning. Numerous articles and books have been devoted to an analysis of the factors which influence learning and the elaboration of processes by which learning seems most likely to be enhanced.

Methodology and Learning. Learning has been defined as a consistent change in behavior which, in educational institutions, is brought about by the activities and experiences that are provided by the school. Keeton, in a publication of the Association for Higher Education, realistically proposed that "Courses define only part of the climate of learning, perhaps a minor part." With respect to instructional method, he suggested that ". . . preoccupation with methods of teaching, unless informed by a comprehensive theory about the climate of learning within which they are applied, may prove to be a wasted effort."[3]

Thus, it should be emphasized that teaching methods, procedures, and techniques are not an end in themselves, but are rather a means by which students can be assisted to solve their individual and social problems. They involve the planning and arrangement of experiences which facilitate the complex process known as learning.

It has been demonstrated that the motivated student learns more readily and permanently than an unmotivated one. Cronbach strongly related motivation to the instructional situation and the role of the teacher:

> The problem in motivation is not to awaken an inert audience, but to direct the energy of an alert group into constructive channels and keep it there. Enthusiasm from the teacher helps sell the goals of the classroom.[4]

---

[3] Morris Keeton, "The Climate of Learning in College," *College and University Bulletin, 15*: 1-2, 5-6, Nov. 15, 1962, p. 1.

[4] Lee J. Cronbach, *Educational Psychology,* 2nd ed. (New York: Harcourt, Brace & World, Inc., 1963) p. 498.

Some Principles of Learning. The modern teacher is confronted with the difficult task of selecting and applying those concepts of learning which seem most personally satisfying, philosophically consistent, and educationally sound. Most teachers may eventually develop a psychology of learning which is, in actuality, a composite of many theories. Such an approach characteristically has been described as eclectic.

Despite the confusion which is still very much apparent concerning the learning process, certain basic relationships have emerged and have been generally adopted in recent years. The following principles are among the more prominently accepted in keeping with modern educational psychology. Learning is most effective when:

The learning objectives and philosophy of the program are planned and clearly understood by both the teacher and the student.

Reciprocal respect and a friendly emotional atmosphere exists between the teacher and the learner.

The student has meaningful, satisfying, and realistic goals which guide his learning activities.

Motivation is provided through a regard for the needs, interests, problems, and concerns of the learner.

An attractive, aesthetic, safe, and healthful environment is provided.

Learners are carefully studied by the teacher and provision is made for individual differences.

The learning activities and experiences are supplemented and enriched by the use of related materials.

A tolerance for failure is developed through the provision of a backlog of successes.

The learner engages in active, real-life experiences which are related to one another and to the problems of home, school, and community.

There is continuous and periodic student and program evaluation.

The need for improvement in the quality of learning rather than in the quantity was pointed out by Tyler. He suggested that "we must set forth the conditions under which learning takes place and then encourage each teacher to use imagination and skill in providing those conditions."[5] Teaching method, of course, provides the vehicle for meeting such an obligation.

Basic Instructional Criteria. Those aspects of teaching and learning which most strongly influence methodology in education have been identified and briefly discussed. It should be apparent that the techniques and procedures of instruction are vitally dependent upon a fundamental understanding of these concepts. As a director of learning, the teacher is professionally and morally obligated to exert every effort toward fulfilling this responsibility. It is generally recognized that no one method or procedure can be effective in all situations or when utilized continuously. Certain fundamental instructional criteria also must be considered before any single technique can be operationally implemented. The selection of any method should adhere to the following educational principles:

Any instructional procedure should be regarded as an educational tool and not merely for the purpose of entertainment.

The technique should be suited to the readiness and the maturity of the group or the grade level using it.

The method of presentation should be guided by the objectives of the subject field, the purposes of the school, and education in general.

Adequate time, space, and equipment should be available to insure effective implementation.

The procedure should provide for sequential growth and development through a planned progression of activities and concepts.

There should be adequate planning and preparation on the part of the teacher in the use of any instructional approach.

The procedure should be of interest and appeal to the learner and considerate of his problems and needs.

------

[5] Ralph W. Tyler, "Conditions for Effective Learning," *NEA Journal*, 48: 47–49, Sep., 1959, p. 47.

The method should utilize or incorporate experiences that assure significance in the thinking and behavior of each learner.

In all instances, the technique or procedure should be a vehicle by which to facilitate definite learning.[6]

A Look Ahead. A brief historical background of educational methodology, the teaching and learning processes, certain instructional criteria, and some principles of planning for teaching were discussed in this chapter. The intent of this treatment was to bring about a recognition that the techniques of instruction cannot be set apart from the factors and conditions which underlie their effective utilization. The teacher of today must understand and keep abreast of current developments in the related scientific fields which contribute to and influence educational practice.

Specific techniques of teaching are discussed in the remainder of this book, which is not proposed to be all-inclusive, although a great many approaches to the instructional situation are presented. All have proved suitable and successful under varying classroom and group circumstances. For functional utilization, the procedures have been described from the viewpoint of the teacher. This should not infer that the learner is only a "receiving" organism.

Certain general considerations, usually involved in the planning and implementation of instruction, and which are common to all techniques, are taken somewhat for granted. It is assumed, for example, that the teacher would attempt to select the procedure most appropriate for a particular situation, insure its compliance with established objectives, and apply proper evaluative devices in appraising the results. With adaptation and application to individual circumstances, the reader should find the ensuing information to be of valuable assistance.

---

[6] Adapted from: Richard K. Means, "Practical Instructional Methods in Health Education," *Journal of School Health*, 28: 223-27, Sept., 1958.

Chapter 2

Group Techniques and Procedures

Mind is the great lever of all things; human thought is the
process by which human ends are ultimately answered.

Daniel Webster

Group membership is an integral part of American life and
this constitutional right of free expression is treasured. Every-
where and every day individuals get together to converse or to deliberate specific problems—in the home, at work, or across the back
fence. Meeting in groups is a natural and common way to exchange
ideas or to attempt to solve problems. In the teaching-learning
situation, there are impressive values to be gained from well-
planned and organized group experiences.

Meaning of Group Procedures. Group procedures include those
activities that involve interaction among learners in cooperative
enterprises. Such experiences might encompass the total class as
a group under student or teacher guidance or involve individuals
in smaller groups.

Values of Group Activity. Productive group work is the result
of careful planning, expert guidance, and appropriate appraisal.
There are numerous benefits to be gained from the employment of
various group procedures under proper conditions. Some of the
more important include:

The quality of individual work is frequently improved by co-operative enterprise.

Leadership is learned through working with others in the attainment of worthwhile group goals.

Group learning, which involves a pooling of knowledge and experience, is often more lasting than individual learning.

The recognition given an individual by peers in a group activity is frequently more meaningful than that afforded by the teacher alone.

The learner is more likely to accept ideas formulated by joint decision than those given by one in a position of authority.

Group activity provides a democratic setting for solving problems and fostering wholesome human relations.

Principles of Effective Group Work. In order for group activity to be effective, certain general principles are basic to its use:

Group work should be favored over other teaching approaches in light of specific outcomes to be derived.

The purposes of any group activity should be established jointly by both students and the teacher.

The group should be able to evaluate objectively its progress at various times in order to determine how well specific objectives are being achieved.

An opportunity should be provided for each member to make some meaningful contribution to the group in keeping with his abilities.

The group should be given ample responsibility and allowed considerable freedom to operate without undue external pressure toward the achievement of its purposes.

Initial experiences of a group nature should be especially carefully planned to insure that they are successful and enjoyable.

Through well developed group experiences, the student can be afforded opportunities to learn not only subject matter, but also the necessary skills of social interaction. The specific group techniques which comprise the remainder of this chapter are potentially valuable in helping to meet these and other instructional objectives.

Brainstorming

Brainstorming is a technique which is valuable for the stimulation and generation of ideas and the facilitation of their expression. The purpose of the procedure is to promote a *quantity* of ideas bearing upon a particular subject by identifying all possible aspects related to it. Brainstorming involves the cooperative thinking by groups toward the solution to a specific problem.

Procedural Steps

Selection of topic: A topic or problem can be selected by the teacher or by the class, but should be one that will elicit good response by the group or groups. It might best be phrased as a question.

Groups: Assign class members to different groups which are arranged to eliminate any unnecessary interference with one another. Effective operational size of each group might vary from as few as six to as many as 18 students.

Group leaders: Appoint or allow each group to select a chairman and one or more secretaries, the number of secretaries depending upon the size of the group. The number should be adequate to assure that all individual responses will be recorded.

Role of leaders: The chairman should maintain only a passive leadership role. He is responsible for keeping the group on the subject, stopping any criticism of ideas, and generally enforcing the rules prescribed for the technique. The secretary or secretaries must record *all* comments that are made by individuals within the group.

Explanation: Define the approach for the class setting forth some anticipated outcomes of the brainstorming session. Identify any problems that might likely be encountered.

General rules: Indicate that all judgments, evaluations, and criticisms should be withheld from the session itself, but might be used in later follow-up discussion. Point out that all statements should be positive in nature; discourage negative comments. Encourage free-wheeling, use of imagination, and additions to the ideas of others. A snapping of fingers during brainstorming is sometimes used to indicate the desire to hitchhike on another's idea.

Statement of topic: Different groups might work with the same or different topics. Insure a clear understanding of the problem by all students. Provide examples where needed to insure comprehension. Allow approximately 30 seconds after the problem has been presented to the group for each individual to organize his thinking on the subject.

Initiation: Begin the discussion by making or by having the chairman make a positive statement relative to the problem. This should serve to stimulate the "train of thought" for the participants.

Involvement: All ideas presented should be recorded by the secretary or secretaries during the discussion. Assist each group as needed, in cooperation with the chairman. The discussion might continue for from five to perhaps 30 minutes, depending upon the nature of the problem, the pace of the group or groups, and the enthusiasm of the participants. A one minute warning signal should be given prior to the lapse of time.

Culmination: After the designated time has elapsed, allow approximately two minutes for each group to categorize its ideas and eliminate any overlapping suggestions. The chairman and other members of the group should assist the secretary in synthesizing key ideas.

Discussion: Discussion might be accomplished under teacher direction or with the active participation of each group chairman. Briefly review and summarize the major ideas presented in the session.

Follow-up: Determine the extent to which objectives were met. Make appropriate application to the work under study. Plan for any follow-up activities which might relate to the lesson. Record any information to be used in evaluation that might have been derived from the experience.

Advantages and Values

Brainstorming:

Stimulates interest, the power of association, a spirit of competition, free use of imagination, and active participation.

Develops an understanding and an appreciation for the thoughts and points of view of others.

Is relatively economical in terms of time, does not necessitate any elaborate classroom arrangements, and can be effectively used with both small and large groups.

Eliminates time-wasting arguments during discussion and encourages participation by all students without the possibility of destructive or cynical criticism by others.

Limitations and Problems

The enthusiasm of individual members could cause the group to get out of hand or the discussion to be monopolized, and necessitate certain control measures.

Successful brainstorming depends in part upon the understanding of the procedure by the participants and the careful selection of a topic and qualified chairman and secretary.

Little evaluation and constructive criticism of individual ideas takes place during the discussion.

The recording of all comments and statements during the session could slow the spontaneous generation of ideas and the overall procedure.

Examples

Under proper conditions, the following questions might be illustrative of the nature of possible topics or problems for brainstorming: In what ways can we protect ourselves from disease? When would an understanding of how to compute interest on money be useful? How has the weather influenced the course of history? Why do we need to know how to speak and write effectively? How are gases and liquids used to do work? Other sessions might be even more creative in nature, such as the naming of a new product or the development of a class theme or special project.

Although brainstorming is a Madison Avenue innovation which has seen extensive utilization in business and industry, the approach has been applied effectively in education. An example of its use by faculty at Wisconsin State College should serve to further describe the technique and indicate certain worthwhile outcomes:

It has been traditional at the Wisconsin college to devote a day or two early each fall to a discussion of some problem facing the institution. . . . the Administrative Council decided to examine the services of the college and see how they could be expanded in three areas—to students, to area schools, and to nearby communities.

Someone suggested the "brainstorming" technique, and . . . the results were rather amazing. Within one hour, a total of 450 suggestions came from six groups. When the duplicates were weeded out and the obviously "impractical" discarded, it was found that there still remained approximately 130 ideas.

That the faculty entered into the spirit of the session is attested by some of the suggestions: an official "date bureau" to serve the college students, a legal "lovers' lane," and a tennis court that converts to an ice rink in the winter time. Perhaps not as farfetched in Wisconsin as it might be in some states was the suggestion that beer be served in the cafeteria.

Faculty members themselves seemed to enjoy the new approach. They felt they became better acquainted in the brainstorming atmosphere than in the more formal committee arrangement. A new member of the staff, who in his previous jobs had suffered through some rather tedious faculty meetings, came prepared to read a novel. At the end of the day, the book remained unopened.[1]

Committee Work

Committee work involves the active participation of individual class members in small group activity. The committee ordinarily consists of from four to 12 or more members and frequently explores phases of a particular problem or topic through the problem solving approach. Committee work is usually an on-going type of experience which may culminate in a project after a designated period of time.

Procedural Steps

Selection of unit: Select several topics or problems which lend themselves to the committee approach, broad enough to facilitate

---

[1] Wayne Wolfe, "A College Faculty's 'Brainstorming'," *School and Society,* 86: 79-80, Feb. 15, 1958.

group investigation, yet specific enough to be functionally productive. Clear purposes for each committee should be formulated in keeping with instructional objectives.

Organization: Discuss the overall committee plan with the group. Identify specific outcomes to be derived. Establish the topics to be investigated. Allow each student to select an area of interest and a committee, or assign each class member to a group. The number of students on each committee would be determined by the topic assigned. A four member committee might be limited in scope and potential while a group of 15 could be unwieldy. Establish a time plan for the committee work.

Initiation: Indicate some organizational structure, yet allow for freedom of suggestion and change. Discuss any further committee organizational factors. Select a chairman and a recorder for each committee. Identify the specific tasks to be performed and provide for the delegation of individual duties. Establish a due date for committee reporting.

Investigation and orientation: Some time should be set aside for member research. Short committee meetings are needed for discussion, organization, analysis, and interpretation. Supervise the action within the groups, offer suggestions, and answer questions. Record committee discussion. Each committee should collect data, analyze applicable information, and reach some conclusions.

Discussion: A limited amount of time should be devoted to the discussion of the major findings, conclusions, and recommendations of each committee. Allow for questions and individual comments. Attempt to consolidate the work of the separate groups and offer general relationships to one another.

Appraisal and application: Summarize the major points made and the important findings of each group. Show the application to the unit under study. Make any appropriate follow-up assignments which might have arisen from the committee work.

Advantages and Values

Committee work:

Fosters growth in leadership qualities and provides opportunities to work as a contributing member of a group.

May be effectively utilized at all grade levels, for various subjects, and with small or relatively large classes.

Encourages creative investigation, critical thinking, and independent observation.

Provides citizenship experience which is valuable as a common element of group interaction in modern society.

Limitations and Problems

Some students, due to a variety of reasons, do not readily or actively respond to this type of group action.

Committee leadership and direction is important in order to avoid the delegation of work to only a few individuals and to prevent duplication of effort.

Hostilities may sometimes develop between individuals within the committee or cliques may form which impede group effort and cooperative action.

There may be unnecessary domination by one or several members of a given committee to the exclusion of others.

Examples

Committees can be an effective procedure for utilization in a variety of situations and for many different subjects. Children in the second grade of a Texas school organized into small committees to construct a community in the classroom. The nature of this activity was revealed by the teacher:

> The committees worked with persistence. The art committee undertook heavy responsibility in working out a pattern for the walls and painting appropriate pictures for the board behind the community center. The book committee assembled a book of stories for us to read and dramatize. The health committee found charts on proper foods and checked the grocery store to see if the groceryman was "on his toes." The program committee presented a program each Friday afternoon, composed of something interesting we had found out during the week. The health committee encouraged us to keep our streets and homes clean. The policeman and his committee helped us in securing our wraps and getting in and out of the building. . . .

The second-grade room had truly become theirs, and not just a place where they had to spend so many hours each day.[2]

Problem Solving

Problem solving is a complex integration of many kinds of responses that vary from one situation to another and take many different forms. It is not an isolated and unitary process, but rather one that seeks new ways, modifications, and patterns of behavior in attaining a goal. It involves the presentation and analysis of a real or hypothetical problem to arouse curiosity, interest, and student activity which culminates in a scientifically determined conclusion or solution.

Procedural Steps

Initiation: Keep in mind that problem solving commonly entails seven basic procedures which govern its operation. These are readily adaptable to the instructional situation and are identified and elaborated upon in the following steps.

Selection of problem: The problem selected should be relevant to the needs, interests, and concerns of the group and appropriate to the unit under study. Once determined, the problem is frequently formulated into question form. It should be capable of solution and possess a worthwhile goal which can be attained. A real life situation or a current problem often meets the necessary requisites.

Definition: Insure that the problem is clearly understood by all students. Anticipate any sub-problems that exist or are likely to arise. Work out a practical plan of procedures to be followed. Provide for a functional division of labor to investigate different aspects of the problem. Present, illustrate, and clearly explain the important dimensions of the problem and the general process of problem solving.

Collection of data: Significant related facts and pertinent information should be assembled by the students before discussion.

---

[2] Association for Supervision and Curriculum Development, 1949 Yearbook, *Toward Better Teaching* (Washington: The Association, 1949), pp. 66-67.

Assist in the location and use of important sources of information. Recall previously acquired information which might be helpful toward a solution to the problem. Determine what additional information and data are needed. Select and organize all pertinent data.

Interpretation of data: Provide for open communication between all class members. Be well informed concerning the problem and well acquainted with all related data and factual information. Carefully study and analyze the assembled data with respect to their value in relation to the problem.

Conclusions: Identify and examine possible conclusions which might be drawn from the data collected. Consider ways in which the problem might be solved in keeping with the information gathered and evaluated. Discuss the conclusions and attempt to reach a logical and reasonable decision.

Application: Make application of the selected conclusions to the solution to the problem. Develop a procedure for testing each conclusion. Eliminate those conclusions which are least reliable or impractical following testing. Reconsider the remaining conclusions and suggest others which might have developed in light of new information.

Evaluation: Make a detailed appraisal of the results. Evaluation should actually be a continuous process throughout the entire problem solving experience. Finalize ideas and conclusions which relate to a solution. Consider other follow-up activities related to the problem.

Advantages and Values

Problem solving:

Contributes to the development of reflective thinking, creative expression, critical analysis, and logical reasoning.

May be effectively utilized to help solve class problems and meet prevailing group needs.

Capitalizes on the natural interest possessed by students in dealing with concerns that are commensurate with their abilities.

May provide valuable carry-over benefits with respect to an application to future individual and group problems.

Limitations and Problems

Problem solving demands a great deal of teacher effort, preparation, time, imagination, and skill in group control.

The problem solving approach requires a wise selection of topic, a timely application of content, and a shrewd judgment of human behavior.

The actual work in problem solving may be accomplished by only a few class members unless all students are properly motivated to actively participate.

Problem solving can sometimes be highly confusing and frustrating unless the procedures are carefully defined and understood.

Examples

The ability to solve problems is one of the major objectives of instruction. Sound problem solving results in genuine quantitative thinking. Learning opportunities for such expression exist in every subject area.

The more complex and refined characteristics of the problem solving approach were suggested by Manning. In relation to safety in the elementary school, he described the ensuing circumstances:

> The teacher and the class study their school environment for accident-laden situations. They carefully observe these situations, thoughtfully discuss and analyze them, and then propose what seem to be the most promising means of eliminating or guarding against them. Notice how closely the procedure parallels the approach of the scientist, and how such thinking has been directed at a realistic and vital problem that is of genuine concern to the participants.

> Each time a major accident occurs, the routine machinery of the classroom comes to a halt and the accident comes to the top of the agenda. The class may go out to the scene of the accident for first-hand investigation, and then come back to their room where the sequence and conditions are reenacted. The children attempt to analyze the cause and to make suitable recommendations. The process is calm, objective, and analytical. It is

scientific thinking in action directed at a highly meaningful
situation in the children's own lives.[3]

Other Group Procedures

Buzz Session. The buzz session is a group activity designed to
divide a large class into smaller groups for discussion purposes.
The designated groups ordinarily are composed of from five to
eight members, depending upon the size of the class. The buzz
session can be effectively used to deal with difficult questions,
problems, or controversial issues. It involves discussion for a limited period of time and is sometimes called a sub-discussion or
cluster group.

Case Study. Case studies possess many of the essentials of problem solving. They entail the use of detailed research of individual
situations as a basis for instruction and the development of principles of action. They are based upon a thorough investigation of
a "case" in order to shed light upon the background, circumstances,
and relationships. Factual experiences of the instructor, student,
another person, or a fictitious character may be utilized.

Colloquium. The colloquium technique involves the use of two
panels—one consisting of authoritative resource persons and the
other of selected class members. It permits direct class participation on an equal status with the invited "experts." A moderator
ordinarily is utilized to guide the discussion, direct pertinent questions, and encourage panel and audience participation as desired.

Debate. The debate consists of a clear-cut pro and con discussion
of a question or issue. It is conducted according to an extremely
definitive set of rules which is followed closely by the participants.
It pairs several speakers on each side that have a definite responsibility to perform in support of a given proposition. The debate is
actually a specialized form of persuasion dealing with some specific resolution.

Discussion. A discussion involves the verbal interaction of a
number of individuals who perceive one another as participants in
a common activity. It is a socializing procedure designed to utilize

---

[3] Duane Manning, *The Qualitative Elementary School* (New York: Harper
& Row, Publishers, 1963) p. 36.

cooperative oral participation toward the resolution of a particular problem or question. A discussion may proceed with or without active leader direction, although it usually requires some degree of moderation to guide group thinking effectively.

Forum. A forum consists of two or more presentations to a group on the same subject or topic with audience participation. It basically is used to present opposing sides of a controversial question or issue and is followed by a question and answer period directed to the speakers. It differs from debate in that no attempt is made to discredit a particular viewpoint but rather merely to consider the various aspects of the issue.

Panel Discussion. The panel discussion is a conversational exchange of ideas by selected participants on a topic, problem, question, or issue. It is a relatively informal oral process which brings together individuals who possess differing points of view concerning a subject of mutual interest providing ample latitude for exploration and discussion. Opposing panels sometimes are utilized with question and answer exchanges.

Sociogram. The sociogram is a chart device which indicates certain relationships between individuals in a group at a particular time and under a given set of circumstances. Although perhaps not technically a "group technique" it has been included here because it is designed to elicit responses which might be used to foster a greater understanding of individual problems and class attitudes, practices, and interactions.

Symposium. The symposium ordinarily consists of two or more relatively brief presentations to a group which deal with different specific phases of the same general subject. The presentations usually are followed by some audience participation in the form of questions or discussion. It often is used in place of the lecture approach and provides for greater involvement and wider participation.

Workshop. A workshop is a group gathering in which individuals attack and study problems. In a classroom setting, workshop activities often are specifically planned and organized by students and conducted under teacher guidance. The technique also frequently is used as an in-service improvement procedure for teachers, administrators, and other school personnel.

Chapter 3

Dramatic Techniques and Procedures

The power of imagination makes us infinite.

John Muir

Students, particularly younger children, have a natural inclination to mimic, to act out, and to engage in other forms of dramatic activity. When properly planned and controlled, such behavior fosters greater appreciation and understanding of our world. Dramatic activity is a valuable learning opportunity for both the participant and the observer. Every student in the classroom can obtain meaning from any of the various dramatic techniques utilized in instruction. Such techniques add interest, clarity, enrichment, and zest to the learning process.

Meaning of Dramatization. The word "drama" is derived from the Greek "to do or to act." Dramatization may take many forms, ranging from the short ad-libbed skit to the detailed and carefully rehearsed full-length play.

Values of Dramatic Experiences. Drama possesses a number of characteristics which makes it a valuable asset in the learning situation. It is motivating to students and may contribute greatly to total development through a number of incidental values.

Hartley, Frank, and Goldenson identified eight related func-

27

tions or values of dramatization. They proposed the following with specific reference to the preschool or kindergarten situation:

> Through this activity the child is given an opportunity to imitate adults; play out real life roles in an intense way; reflect relationships and experiences; express pressing needs; release unacceptable impulses; reverse roles usually taken; mirror growth; and to work out problems and experiment with solutions.[1]

Dramatization as an educational procedure is valuable for conveying information, developing understandings, and communicating key ideas. It can serve effectively to stimulate student participation and facilitate spontaneity and emotional expression.

Principles of Effective Dramatic Participation.   For most desirable results, certain basic procedures should precede the classroom drama. The following considerations are suggestive of evaluative criteria which might be applied by the teacher:

Plan the dramatization so that it progresses logically and smoothly for the period of time designated.

Tie the content or subject matter into other work under study and to problems of real-life value.

Actively involve as many participants as possible in different dramatizations which might be developed over a period of time.

Create an active interest on the part of the observers as well as the participants.

Avoid busy-work type activities, such as the construction of elaborate scenery or costumes, unless they can be justified as meaningful educational experiences.

Role Playing

Role playing is the spontaneous acting out of a situation. It is a form of improvisation in which the participants assume the identity of other persons and then react as they perceive their

---

[1] Ruth E. Hartley, Laurence K. Frank, and Robert M. Goldenson, *Understanding Children's Play* (New York: Columbia University Press, 1952) p. 27.

behavior in a particular set of circumstances. Spontaneity and invention characterize role playing with an emphasis upon individual performance and the role itself, rather than a coordinated group experience centered on the problem.

Procedural Steps

Selection of topic: The problem should concern itself in some way with the unit of work under study, and should deal with a significant idea, concept, or issue involving personalities in a natural real life situation. The problem selected should encourage the involvement of feelings and attitudes rather than straight factual information. Think in terms of a situation that necessitates a minimum of participants and that is relatively simple to portray, making sure that the problem lies within the experience of the group.

Preplanning: Develop several ideas for motivating the group to participate with enthusiasm. Carefully define the problem and the roles to be represented in its enactment. Plot a simple drama in general terms and attempt to anticipate how it might proceed. Identify certain students who might be invited to participate as role players. Plan for some informality but with learning as the primary objective.

Creation of atmosphere: The class might be encouraged to assist in the formulation of the problem. Small groups might be designated to help set up the incident and to define general methods of procedure. Identify the specific roles necessary to portray the situation. Describe briefly the roles to be played and provide some limited background regarding the personalities and attitudes to be demonstrated. Indicate the time to be allotted—five to ten minutes of actual role playing time is frequently used. A story or simple plot might be used to introduce the situation.

Selection of individuals: Allow for some participation by the group in the selection of role characters. Volunteers might be enlisted. Two to five players usually are considered desirable for a single episode. Provide a name for each character to be portrayed. Certain players may be sent from the room while specific points are being discussed. This helps to avoid any distortion or coloring of the roles to be played.

Preparation: A short warm-up period might be provided for

the participants, but any memorization or rehearsal should be discouraged. Introduce the situation to the group that will be observing and alert them to things to look for in the presentation. Specific observers might be assigned to watch particular roles for key ideas.

Involvement: Begin the role playing. The roles should be portrayed as the characters perceive them and as the plot develops. A tape recorder might be used to capture the drama and to provide a basis for later discussion. The teacher might halt the episode whenever there are main ideas to be emphasized. Following the initial presentation, the roles might be reversed. The same set of players or another group of participants might portray the same roles in order to characterize different ways of behaving in a similar situation.

Culmination: Halt the role playing at the end of the specified time or when the dramatization begins to lag. Thank the participants for their performances and allow them to engage in the discussion which should follow.

Discussion: Attempt to identify the main ideas and emotional reactions presented. Allow for class involvement through questions, comments, and observations. Obtain the reactions of the role players as well as any specific observers. Summarize the key points and clarify what was learned. Indicate the consequences of certain actions if carried to a conclusion different than that portrayed. Attempt to arrive at some solution or plan of possible procedure for solving the problem or for handling similar situations.

Evaluation: Note ways in which the role playing might have been improved. Tactfully discuss any glaring mistakes or omissions. Provide further student activities related to the role playing or that might have resulted from the experience.

Advantages and Values

Role playing:

Is fun, interesting, motivating, meaningful, and helps to thwart the routine of other types of learning experiences.

Provides insight into common individual and group problems, reveals different attitudes, and tests various ideas in a practical situation.

Encourages student creativity, self-confidence, poise, self-reliance, cooperation, and courtesy.

Requires relatively little special preparation and utilizes the dramatic instinct which is possessed by most students in some measure.

May reveal student feelings and attitudes about adults through their identification with them.

Limitations and Problems

Role playing participants are sometimes unable to identify realistically with the character and the behavior sought in a given situation.

An overemphasis might be placed on the actual performance to the neglect of the underlying purpose of the technique.

Misguided humor or student mockery could disrupt the experience unless it is carefully planned and executed.

Role playing is time consuming and somewhat limited by class size, although it can be used effectively with large groups.

The talented and gregarious personality has a tendency to monopolize the activity unless proper guidance and orientation is provided.

Examples

Role playing can be applied as an instructional technique in many different instances.

Telephone conversations between different individuals: A boy asking a girl for a date, a complaint to a business establishment concerning an inferior product that was purchased, or reaction to a wrong number call which came when one was asleep or in the bathtub. *Various social situations*: Introducing parents to a classmate, accepting an invitation to a dance, or making a graceful exit from a party. *Different ways of expressing conflict or frustration*: Illustrating rationalization, displacement, regression, and other defense or escape mechanisms of behavior. The group might be asked to identify and discuss these various roles and their implications. *Leadership situations:* Presiding at a meeting as chairman, serving as team captain of a sport or game, or assigning undesirable tasks to employees in the capacity of the "boss."

Grambs and Iverson told how one teacher used role playing to show the class how different people assist or impede the process of group thinking. They provided the following analysis of the situation:

> A teacher had been concerned about some of the group projects in her class. Several of the groups were working very well together, but in two groups there was dissension due to dominating leadership as well as to disagreement over what the group was trying to do. Therefore, at the beginning of one class hour, the teacher said that she was going to ask several members of the class to be a "pretend" group. She called up five students and gave each a separate slip of paper, cautioning them not to tell anyone what was on the paper. The slips were as follows:
>
> 1. You are very eager to be chairman of the group.
> 2. You don't like anything that is suggested.
> 3. You are very enthusiastic about almost any project suggested.
> 4. You refuse to take sides in a discussion.
> 5. You are eager to see the group working together on almost anything.
>
> She then asked the students to pretend that they were a group similar to one in class and gave them a project to plan that paralleled those being worked on. The students threw themselves into the roles with great vigor, to the amusement and chagrin of various of the class members who saw their own group roles being portrayed.[2]

Sociodrama

The sociodrama is an unrehearsed and spontaneous dramatization dealing with some problem or issue of significance in a social relations situation. By contrast with the individual role emphasis in role playing, sociodrama is characterized by attention to social problems which are acted out by the group. It is an especially valuable technique for studying contemporary affairs, history, civics, and other similar subjects.

---

[2] Jean D. Grambs and William J. Iverson, *Modern Methods in Secondary Education* (New York: Holt, Rinehart and Winston, Inc., 1952), pp. 195-96.

Procedural Steps

Identification of problem: The problem or issue to be considered should deal with some important social idea involving personality relationships. Class members might be asked to name problems in social relations which they would like to have solved or to name situations which bother them. Select a topic that lends itself to analysis in a re-created experience.

Definition: The problem or situation should be appropriate to the unit of study, and should be simple, yet comprehensive enough to be educationally sound. Identify the general plot and the characters to be involved. Attempt to lead the class to a visualization of the situation.

Selection of participants: The characters should be selected from volunteers in light of the teacher's understanding of the class, the individual, and group needs. Describe each character in connection with the problem or situation. Identify the roles in the situation and describe the personal feelings and consequent actions of participants which are to be involved. Permit the "actors" to briefly rehearse and agree upon the setting and action to be taken.

Preparation: Orient the class to the problem or situation. This might be done during the time that the participants are briefly concentrating on their individual roles. The situation should then be discussed with the total group. Small group sociodramas also might be conducted which involve all class members at the same time.

Presentation: A sociodrama presentation ordinarily lasts for about five to 10 minutes of actual activity. Introduce the characters and their roles. Allow time for the acting out of the situation without undue interruption. The teacher should assume a backseat role and not intrude so long as the action moves forward in relation to the problem. At an opportune time, or when the drama begins to lag, the sociodrama may be ended.

Discussion: Allow adequate time for general discussion from both the class and the participants. Provide for comments and questions. Part or all of the sociodrama might feasibly be repeated with the same or different players.

Advantages and Values

Sociodrama:

Is an effective tool for stimulating and motivating the exploration and refinement of student experience in a wide variety of social situations.

Assists the teacher and student in gaining insight into feelings, attitudes, and social behavior.

Provides for tailoring of situations and roles related to almost any grade level, size group, or field of study.

Facilitates a more objective observation and analysis of student behavior since the situation is simulated and not as emotionally strained as a real life circumstance might be.

Can be used to help develop desirable social skills and behavior patterns, such as loyalty, honesty, leadership, cooperation, and social responsibility.

Limitations and Problems

Sociodrama is exceedingly time consuming for best results in terms of planning, preparation, organization, presentation, and evaluation.

Sometimes there is a tendency in sociodrama for the players to imitate themselves rather than to project into the situation as the role might demand.

The sociodrama needs to be carefully appraised in relation to distinct educational value and should probably be used sparingly.

Examples

There are several major types of sociodrama situations which are commonly referred to as the life problem, the problem story, and the social issue approaches. The following topics or situations should serve to exemplify some of the possibilities: the issue of universal military training, the great debate over the provisions of the United States Constitution in 1787, social problems leading to the French Revolution, difficulties facing an immigrant, and how to apply for a job.

Wood reported a concrete sociodrama problem concerned with honesty which was proposed by her students. Jim and George, both nine years of age, took some candy in a grocery store and left without paying for it. The clerk saw them and called George's mother. When the boys arrived at George's home both mothers were waiting for them. Within this setting the class was asked what they thought occurred at George's home. According to Wood, two sociodramas were developed to deal with the problem in honesty. In the first George was given a sound scolding by his mother, but nothing else. In the second he was required to return to the store to pay for the candy. The class discussed both situations, decided which solution was best, and thus established a rule of conduct.[3]

Storytelling

Storytelling is the narration to a class of incidents or events, which may be true or fictitious, and read, told, or presented through various forms of expression. Its general aim is to present a message, interpret the literature, or inspire reading and expression. The procedure can be used to initiate new units of study, foster imagination, build new vocabulary, create a sense of reality, stimulate creativeness, and to provide a common background experience for the development of ideas.

Procedural Steps

Selection of story: The story should possess substance and involve content related to the unit of study. It should be viewed as a distinct learning experience with clearly formulated objectives. Numerous sources of excellent stories are available or the story can be teacher or student developed.

Rehearsal: Preview the story in detail so as to know it well. Avoid rote memorization. Attempt to create a visual picture of the story and project into its character. Consider various ways in which effectiveness might be enhanced.

Preparation: Select and arrange any supplementary materials

---

[3] Mildred W. Wood, "Role-Playing: Effective in Family Relationship Units," *Clearing House,* 26:469-71, Apr., 1952.

which will be used. Arrange the seating to facilitate as close an association between the storyteller and the listener as is possible. Attempt to provide an eye level relationship with any visual materials that are to be used.

Introduction: Motivate the group to listen attentively to the story. The introduction of the lesson is vital to its success. Use an "eye-catching" or "ear-catching" technique to insure initial attention. Student participation through questions or an open-end statement are useful.

Presentation: Provide for a simple and direct narration of the story. Present it naturally but dramatically and enthusiastically. Use normal gestures, facial expressions, and different voice inflections. Avoid interrupting the story unnecessarily, but generally allow for some student reaction and response. Note the effect of the materials being used to help present the story.

Discussion: Utilize various techniques to judge the performance in terms of learning. Class discussion, buzz sessions, questions, oral or written tests, and other procedures might prove effective. Provide for further follow-up activities emanating from the story, such as creative writing or individual drawing or construction work. Record information related to the experience for future use.

Advantages and Values

Storytelling:

Provides a natural and realistic charm that grasps student attention, intensifies interest, and generates an enthusiasm for learning.

Encourages the development of good listening skills and provides for aesthetic enjoyment.

Stimulates the imagination and provides opportunities for creative expression.

Creates a concrete situation in which ideas and judgments can be tested and application made to personal experiences.

Limitations and Problems

Inattention, restlessness, and discipline problems may arise during the storytelling process unless there is an adequate understanding of student attention span, principles of learning, and control procedures.

A great deal of imagination, ingenuity, and skill is required to present a story effectively.

Storytelling sometimes introduces unfamiliar words or expressions which may confuse or distort learning unless they are carefully clarified.

There is a tendency to present too many illustrations, examples, or details when telling a story which unnecessarily interrupts or detracts from learning.

Examples

An adaptation of the storytelling art that is frequently used involves the utilization of supplementary materials. Manning described this approach in the following manner:

> In each classroom children were asked to bring a picture of their own choosing to the "reading group." There the teacher invited comment about each picture, and together, she and the child decided on a story to be written on the picture. The rest of the children watched eagerly as they saw the speech of one child take form on his picture. They participated by helping the teacher decide about initial sounds, capital letters, and punctuation.[4]

Other Dramatic Procedures

Game. A game is an educational play situation possessing some structure by virtue of a set of rules or procedures to be followed. Games may require varying degrees of skill, concentration, and coordination, depending upon their organization and execution.

Pageant. A pageant is a type of community drama usually produced out of doors. It commonly is based on local history and frequently associated with some kind of special occasion. Various musical devices, humor, commentators, and other variations of theatrical art sometimes are used.

---

[4] Duane Manning, *The Qualitative Elementary School* (New York: Harper & Row, Publishers, 1963), p. 81.

Pantomime. The pantomime is a variation of role playing, socio-drama, and similar dramatic techniques. It differs in that gestures, facial expressions, and overt movements take the place of spoken words in the portrayal of character roles and situations. Sometimes an unobserved announcer is used to briefly describe the action as it occurs. The pantomime is a valuable way to demonstrate the "right and wrong" or "do and don't" of a situation which involves feeling and action.

Play. A play ordinarily is defined as a carefully rehearsed dramatization that involves a predetermined script, costumed performers, and rather elaborate scenery. It can be extremely useful in portraying important concepts particularly of a social nature. Play scripts are available in printed form from a number of sources or may be developed as a class project.

Projection. The projective procedure involves the use of a stimulus to encourage spontaneous and uninhibited discussion or reaction to social, personal, or real-life problems or situations. It is used to reveal attitudes, beliefs, ideas, and adjustments related to specific problem situations. Open-end or association techniques usually are utilized as stimuli, such as completing a sentence or story, responding to a word or phrase, or describing a picture or symbol.

Psychodrama. Psychodrama is the unrehearsed and spontaneous acting out by an individual of a personally perplexing problem. It has been successfully used as a diagnostic and therapeutic device for understanding and dealing with mental and emotional problems. Psychodrama has educational value in the school in helping to resolve personal conflicts and in demonstrating appropriate responses to problems.

Puppet. Puppets are small figures or dolls. Marionettes are constructed with jointed limbs that can be manipulated from above by attached strings or wire. Hand puppets are made from cloth or paper and are pulled down over the hand. Movement of the hand gives movement and expression.

Rhymes and Jingles. Rhymes and jingles represent a creative writing experience involving the manipulation of words to produce a form of rhythmic meaning. When used sparingly and with discretion the approach provides personal satisfaction, serves to emphasize important points, and motivates the development of certain basic writing skills.

Skit or Playlet. The skit or playlet is a relatively brief dramatic presentation. It frequently is designed to provide a learning opportunity through a planned and rehearsed satirical, comic, or humorous story. The skit or playlet often is used as a tool in the exploration of problems in human relations.

Songs. Songs are musical compositions involving a pattern or combination of rhythmic and melodic tones which are ordinarily aesthetically appealing. Applied to the instructional situation, songs usually are quite simple in structural form and utilized most frequently in the lower grades. They have strong motivational value in learning due to their emotional impact and expression of feeling.

Tableau. The term "tableau" is derived from a French word meaning picture. The tableau is a picturelike scene composed of individuals arranged against some kind of a background. It is a motionless as well as silent portrayal of an event, circumstance, or situation.

Chapter 4

Student Oriented Techniques and Procedures

Nothing has such power to broaden the mind as the ability to investigate systematically and truly all that comes under thy observation in life.

Marcus Aurelius Antoninus

Student activity and involvement do not necessarily produce optimum learning. Active participation by the learner, however, does contribute in many instances to educational achievement. Many objectives established for the school can best be met through the techniques of teaching which recognize and intimately involve the student. Many kinds of student centered activity will result in learning when properly planned and organized. This chapter is concerned with some of those techniques and procedures which most specifically involve the learner.

Values of Student Oriented Procedures. Both the teacher and the student are directly involved in the teaching-learning process. Cooperative planning and student participation in instructional situations are likely to contribute to learning in many different ways. McKean identified nine such values. He proposed that cooperative planning will:

Help students and teacher to understand each other better.

Provide alignment of assignments and classwork with student goals and purposes.

Foster better adaptation to individual differences.

Develop greater student involvement in curricular determination.

Encourage students to accept more responsibility for learning.

Provide a better classroom climate for learning.

Open the way for more opportunity for cooperative student work.

Place more emphasis upon question-answering and problem-solving.

Result in greater learning satisfaction to the learner.[1]

Learning from Experience. Woodruff devoted a chapter of a recent book to how one learns from experience which provided some direction for the development and use of student oriented procedures of instruction. "Our experiences with the world," he asserted, "register within us in the form of concepts, values, and feelings for things, language, skills, and habits. They then become the controlling elements in determining what we try to do, and how well we do it." He proposed the following supporting concepts in relation to this idea:

> When through experience we get a mental picture in our minds of one of the objects or forces which make up our world, we have a concept, which immediately becomes our "set" for any further perception of that same thing.
>
> While concepts are forming through experience, the individual is also learning what value each of the objects and forces has for him through his impressions of how each of them affects him. This sense of value becomes a part of each concept and determines how he feels about it. This tends to influence his behavior toward that thing.
>
> As a concept forms in our minds we learn symbols for the whole concept and for each of its parts or qualities, and these symbols become part of the concept also.

---

[1] Robert C. McKean, *Principles and Methods in Secondary Education* (Columbus, Ohio: Charles E. Merrill Publishing Company , 1962), pp. 145-46.

As we perform muscular actions we develop some degree of skill which can be raised or lowered, depending on use and practice.

When we respond to a recurring situation by performing a given action time after time without variation, that response tends to become automatic or habitual. It will soon occur without our attention, taking place every time its regular cue is present.[2]

Creative Writing

Creative writing is a type of composition involving some degree of self-initiative, spontaneity, and exercise of the imagination by the writer. It may take various forms such as short stories, verse, drama, and other means of self-expression.

Procedural Steps

Subject: Select the area of study to be pursued. Consider various approaches which might be used to stimulate creative writing. Define the purpose of the experience and identify certain potential outcomes.

Pre-planning: Several different techniques might be used to motivate the students. The open-end approach is particularly good— show a part of a film, read a portion of a story, or tell a narrative, leaving the ending up to the student to complete. Pictures and other visual aids might be effectively used to initiate ideas for writing. Select the best procedure and outline the steps to be followed.

Introduction: Clearly identify the topic to be treated and the way in which it relates to the content under study. Provide the lead sentence, the title, or other directional clues to stimulate and initiate the experience. Insure that all students understand their responsibilities. Set forth a definite time limit or due date for the collection of all written materials.

Student writing: Assure that all students get under way as soon as possible. Assist the class as a group and students individually as

---

[2] Asahel D. Woodruff, *Basic Concepts of Teaching,* concise ed. (San Francisco: Chandler Publishing Co., 1961) p. 63.

needed. Answer any questions that might arise. Provide further clues or ideas for those students having difficulty. Provide adequate time to complete the assignment either in class or at home.

Review: Obtain the compositions from each student at the designated time. Carefully read and comment upon each paper. Analyze the reports in keeping with the pre-established objectives and the nature of the assignment. Identify those compositions that will provide for optimum discussion or that illustrate desirable points which should be analyzed. Attempt to include as many students as possible in some manner.

Discussion: Provide a general analysis of all the papers. Bring out key points which should be emphasized. Show important relationships to previous and current work. Develop major concepts. Select certain students to read portions or all of their compositions or personally read or report orally on selected papers. Provide a summary of the compositions.

Evaluation: Distribute all corrected papers. Indicate the nature of all comments. Identify common errors of writing. Grammar, spelling, writing style, sentence structure, and English usage should be mentioned but probably not emphasized in keeping with the general purpose of creative writing.

Advantages and Values

Creative writing:

Provides a realistic opportunity to express inner feelings, original ideas, and imaginative thought.

Helps to develop skills of word selection, verbal expression, organization, and logical development.

Is easily adapted for use with all subject matter at any grade level and easily may be used in combination with a variety of other learning experiences to enrich student experiences.

Provides a stimulus for creative expression and facilitates the release of tensions and frustrations.

Limitations and Problems

The teacher must be imaginative and able to project ideas skillfully along creative lines in order to guide students successfully in their efforts.

The use of creative writing is time consuming and demands a good deal of teacher effort in guidance, analysis, and appraisal.

Creative writing experiences can become a poor substitute for other more productive learning activities unless properly planned, organized, and implemented.

There is a distinct tendency to overemphasize the mechanics of writing to the exclusion or sublimation of creativeness and spontaneity.

Examples

The use of pictures and other visual aids to stimulate and initiate a creative writing experience has proved successful. Contrasting and "cause and effect" relationships easily may be demonstrated through such stimuli. One picture, for example, might indicate a small boy playing in the water on a cold day. A second picture might show the same boy lying in bed obviously suffering from a respiratory ailment. The students might be asked to respond to the query, "What happened?"

An interesting approach to creative writing was described in a recent book by Manning. He provided some detailed suggestions regarding the use of the procedure as follows:

> A primary teacher took her children to the top of a small hill overlooking the village to prime them for a creative writing lesson. The lazy little community stretched out along a forked stream and was very picturesque. The children had never seen their village "from the top side" before and were impressed by the difference in the view. Later, they returned to the classroom to write about what they had seen. At this point their teacher used a rather novel mechanical procedure.

> On the board she had written each letter of the alphabet in both small and capital letters. When a child asked how to spell a word he wished to use in his writing she freely supplied it for him and wrote it on the board under the correct letter. For instance if a child asked for the spelling of "beautiful" she wrote it for him on the board under the letter "b." She freely supplied the spellings because she felt that if she did not the child might substitute a word like pretty which he could spell instead of looking up the word he wanted in the dictionary. The net result

of such substitutions would be to impoverish and detract from the quality of the writing.[3]

Laboratory Experimentation

Laboratory experimentation involves an operation or series of tests undertaken to discover an underlying principle or to prove or disprove a specific point. It generally attempts to demonstrate how things are done, how they work, or some known truth. The technique involves experimental study related to or based on experience. It has the purpose of illustrating and thus helping a group or an individual to understand the content or concept under consideration.

Procedural Steps

Selection: The experiment usually should relate directly to the unit under study and be an integral part of the planned program. Certain specific objectives best may be met by the experimental approach. Insure that the anticipated experiment does not conflict with school policy or law. Available equipment and supplies will determine, of course, the type and extent of the experiment to be conducted.

Approach: An experiment may be conducted in a variety of ways. The teacher may demonstrate the procedure in front of the class, the group may participate in one or more phases of the experiment, or the class may be involved in each step of the process in small groups or individually. Some experiments require several days or weeks in which to be completed. Insure that the necessary equipment and materials are available. Outline in detail the steps to be followed and the expected outcomes to be derived.

Rehearsal: Obtain and set up the necessary equipment and materials for the experiment prior to the time it is to be conducted. Follow each step as set forth in the pre-planning phase, if possible. Make any necessary changes or improvements in the procedures to be followed. Record any additional observations or comments which might have originally been overlooked. Check the results

---

[3] Duane Manning, *The Qualitative Elementary School* (New York: Harper & Row, Publishers, 1963), p. 59.

for reliability and validity. Anticipate and prepare for any questions which might likely be asked.

Orientation: Prepare and arrange all equipment and materials before class begins. Orient the class to the laboratory experimentation approach. It might be important that each student wear old clothes or bring special materials to class. Procure any volunteers who might be needed in conducting the experiment.

Introduction: Clearly identify the problem, indicate the general procedures to be followed, and the apparatus to be used. Discuss the purpose of the experiment and its relationship to the unit under study. Indicate any safety precautions which might need to be considered. Pass out and prepare to use any other materials or equipment which are necessary for the experiment. The objects to be used should be large enough to be observed easily.

Demonstration: Demonstrate the procedures as simply and as rapidly as is feasible. Repeat any steps or procedures that appear unclear. Record the results of the work as the activity proceeds, using graphs, charts, and other appropriate aids. Allow individuals or small groups to try the experiment or parts of it, if possible. Answer any questions that arise during each step of the experiment.

Culmination: Note the results and impact of the experiment on the group. Record any important data. Retest if desirable. Collect, clean, and store or exhibit all equipment and materials which were used.

Discussion: Discuss the outcomes of the experiment and what was learned. Answer student questions and pose others that might have arisen from the demonstration. Identify all key ideas and major concepts. Show any significant relationships to past experiences and to work under study or anticipated. Skillfully summarize the information presented. Make direct application of the main ideas to the work under consideration. Note how the experiment might be improved for future use.

Advantages and Values

Laboratory experimentation:

Provides a clear visual picture and first-hand experience which helps to facilitate the retention of learning.

Allows students the opportunity of working independently, to-gether in groups, or with the teacher, thus providing a common ground of experience leading to the development of responsibility and initiative.

Permits an exposure to laboratory equipment and the scientific method which might result in an increased understanding and appreciation for science.

Might be conducted over any period of time, depending upon the concepts to be learned and the nature of the material being demonstrated.

Can usually be conducted at any desired pace which facilitates questions and answers as the work proceeds and insures greater understanding of the total process.

Limitations and Problems

Safety hazards are inherent in certain experiments, especially those involving the use of chemicals, sharp instruments, fire, breakable objects, or other similar substances or materials.

The results of a given experiment may fail to meet expected outcomes or could be totally unsuccessful.

Experiments sometimes tend to be conducted at advanced levels which do not facilitate easy comprehension by all students.

Some of the better experiments are extremely time consuming, require a good deal of careful planning and preparation, and may actually take weeks to be successfully accomplished.

Laboratory experimentation often necessitates proper equipment, supplies, and facilities which may be expensive, difficult to handle, and hard to store.

Examples

Experimentation procedures can be initiated to illustrate how evaporation takes place, how animal or plant growth and development occurs, how hereditary traits are transmitted, how energy can be changed into useful work, and in general how scientists solve problems.

In a booklet prepared by the American Dental Association, nine different laboratory experiences related to oral health were presented. The following detailed account is concerned with comparative dental anatomy for high school students:

Preparation: Contact veterinarians, dental and medical school laboratories, zoos and biological supply houses in your own or nearby cities and collect the heads of different kinds of animals, such as guinea pigs, rats, rabbits, hamsters, cats, dogs, reptiles and fish. . .

Procedure: Prepare the skulls for study by either of the following methods. (1) Process the head in an autoclave at 121° C. (or in a pressure cooker with about a cup of water at 15 lb. pressure) for at least 30 minutes. Remove the specimens and permit them to cool; then peel the soft tissue from the skull and remove the small particles from the bone with a brush and water. Or (2) cut off gross tissue, empty the cranium, and then boil the specimens in a 5 to 10 per cent aqueous potassium hydroxide solution, (CAUTION: Extreme care should be used to avoid spilling or splashing these highly caustic solutions.) When the bone is free of soft tissue, wash the skulls thoroughly in running water. Residual alkali may be removed by rapidly rinsing the skulls with a dilute solution of acetic acid. Follow this step with a tap water rinse.

Findings: You can now observe the jaw structures, the size and shape of the joint and the kinds and position of the teeth in the jaw. Examine and compare the specimens from the various animals you have selected for your study. Observe and describe the variance of tooth structure among the different species; make comparison and contrast studies. Make drawings of the different parts of the teeth. Study the external and internal structure of the jaws and teeth from different animals and try to show how the structure for each corresponds with the functions performed at the different levels of the natural order of animal life, for example: defense, cutting, chewing food, gnawing wood. Compare tooth structure and the dietary habits of carnivores, herbivores and omnivores.[4]

Survey

A survey involves the investigation and study of specific prob-

---

[4] *Dental Projects for High School Science Students* (Chicago: American Dental Association, 1959), pp. 11-12.

lems or circumstances by means of a scientific process. It consists
of measurement of personal or social attitudes, ideas, or practices
from which a scientific analysis and evaluation can be made. The
survey frequently is used to study individual or group practices,
current program status, or the interrelationships of social process.

Procedural Steps

Exploration: Consult reliable printed sources of information regarding the survey approach. Discuss the procedures involved in
a survey with experts who are familiar with the process. Consider
basic principles of using the survey method. Discuss these principles with the class to insure understanding of the process.

Formulation of a statement: Identify and develop the problem
situation or practice to be surveyed. Some class participation
probably should be enlisted. The problem selected should be timely
and of general interest. It should be one which has not previously
been investigated and one which is capable of solution.

Planning: Determine how and by whom the results are to be
used. Consider the most feasible and economical manner of utilizing class participation. Committees might be used for gathering
data, tabulating the results, and reporting the findings. Enlist the
support of community resources as necessary.

Orientation: Indicate the general procedures to be followed.
Identify and attempt to consider all possible variables which are
likely to be involved. Develop appropriate survey devices as
needed, such as questionnaires or check-lists. Appoint committees
to help facilitate the process.

General rules: Arrange to conduct the survey. Use student
groups to investigate different aspects of the problem. Provide for
group leaders as required. Avoid duplication or repetition of survey visitations or coverage. Insure understanding of specific
responsibilities by students. Provide time for meeting in groups,
discussion, and consolidation of gathered data.

Interpretation: Utilize class participation through discussion or
group work in analyzing the information. Formulate and test
various hypotheses and arrive at general conclusions. Develop
several concrete recommendations as an overall outcome.

Presentation: Use a variety of charts, graphs, and other aids to present the material. List and discuss the major conclusions and recommendations. Compile a written report on the findings where feasible. Related class activities might also be developed to contribute to the survey materials.

Evaluation: Consider the validity and reliability of the results obtained. Indicate ways in which further action might be taken to improve or change existing practices or forms of behavior. Make notes concerning the overall survey process for future reference.

Advantages and Values

Survey:

Provides a face-to-face relationship with public opinion about current issues and their meaning in everyday life.

Discloses local needs and problems which provide insights into community affairs and the responsibilities and obligations of the citizenry.

Is valuable in that it provides for meeting individual differences by virtue of the variety of possible assignments inherent in obtaining survey data.

Helps to illustrate the importance of making sound observations, judgments, and conclusions.

Can serve to provide a valuable source of information and service to the community if properly conducted, analyzed, and reported.

Limitations and Problems

Survey results are sometimes influenced by individual biases, prejudices, and other human expressions which may distort the findings.

The survey sample always should be representative of the group or situation in order for the results to be scientifically accurate and practically useful.

A survey requires considerable teacher and class energy over an extended period of time.

Much of the success of a community survey depends upon other techniques, such as interviews and questionnaires, required in its accomplishment.

It is important to make careful judgments as to what aspects of the survey are to be publicized or reported back to the community.

Examples

The community survey is a means to a variety of exciting and challenging experiences. Among the more specific elements which might be investigated are local problems, practices, or needs related to employment, housing, health and sanitation, safety and accident prevention, industry, business, civic clubs and organizations, and playgrounds and recreation.

A detailed account of a planned four week survey was prepared by Grambs and Iverson. They proposed the following time plan for a full-scale community study:

1ST WEEK: Initiation of survey: student presents visitor, motion picture, or other current provocative material. There is preliminary discussion of the problem and its subproblems. Class study in selected references or text material. Reconsideration of problem areas. First designation of committees . . . Study by groups . . . Reports from groups and plans for further study.

2ND WEEK: Questionnaire group pretests questionnaire. Rest of class continues study. Out-of-class teams assigned. Survey deadline set. . . Interview practice for those who are to use the questionnaire . . . Reports from first interviews. Class evaluates progress. Study continues in broader aspects of problem in text or related references.

3RD WEEK: Class discussion to formulate major ideas of problem area. Quiz: review of material known by class in area. Reports on progress . . . Maps constructed . . . Class evaluates work to date . . . Group assigned to invite community leaders in for final report.

4TH WEEK: Final tabulations: charts and graphs completed. Introduction and background sections written. Class reviews. Class considers data assembled . . . Conclusions agreed upon. . . . Community leaders invited to hear summary and report.

5TH WEEK: Evaluation of total experience. What would we do differently next time? New unit begun.[5]

---

[5] Jean D. Grambs and William J. Iverson, *Modern Methods in Secondary Education* (New York: Holt, Rinehart and Winston, Inc., 1952), pp. 150-51.

Other Student Oriented Procedures

Check list. Check lists are devices used to determine the existence of certain conditions or circumstances. They ordinarily are developed to provide specific information on student behavior, some aspect of the program, or certain qualities of an existing situation. They are completed by merely checking a statement or characteristic which has been determined as important for evaluation. Published check lists are available in many areas of instructional concern or they may be teacher or student constructed.

Collection. Collections may be defined as materials which are gathered individually or by a group that relate to a particular topic or subject. The materials may consist of pictures, maps, clippings, letters, charts, books, stamps, leaves, or other similar specimens or objects. The collected materials usually are arranged in some sequence or order.

Inventory. An inventory is utilized to ascertain the status of an aspect of student behavior, school or community activity, or instructional program. It frequently involves the gathering of information by means of self-appraisal procedures. Many standardized instruments are available in many fields or the inventory device may be teacher or student constructed. The inventory provides a practical base from which to develop instructional, counseling, and guidance programs.

Library Work. Library work involves planned investigation into additional sources of information on a given topic or problem. It is obvious that all the answers to all questions that might arise will not be found in a single reference. Classroom, school, and community libraries provide a ready resource for research. Such reference sources might include encyclopedias, dictionaries, newspapers, books, pamphlets, atlases, magazines, almanacs, and other materials.

Oral Report. The term "oral report" defines itself. Oral reports are assigned easily, can be presented simply in relation to scheduled classroom work, and can be effective with students of all ages. Other instructional materials, such as charts, pictures, slides, photographs, and graphs frequently lend value and sophistication to the report and should be encouraged.

Project. A project may be either an individual or class planned undertaking designed to compile information, collect objects, construct materials, or create something. As a group enterprise, a project might consist of such real-life experiences as purchasing and preparing food for a class luncheon or creating a class newspaper. As an individual learning opportunity, projects might involve painting a mural, writing a story, making clothing, or collecting and mounting different plant or animal specimens.

Questionnaire. The questionnaire is a well-known and frequently used type of survey form. It commonly is utilized to facilitate student opinion studies, self-appraisal procedures, or surveys of a particular curricular activity. Questionnaire results often are used in planning individualized programs to meet specific individual and group needs.

Rating scale. A rating scale is a device that is used for recording the judgments of observations. When properly developed and used it helps to make subjective estimates of a situation, ability, or skill more objective. The rating scale can be used effectively in many different areas of evaluation and may be constructed for specific purposes.

Reading Assignment. Reading assignments enable the learner to journey beyond the confines of the classroom. They merely may involve perusal of a single textbook or go beyond into the vast world of supplementary printed materials. The use of multiple textbooks, typical reference volumes, current media, and student-teacher created materials have value as resources for basic or supportive reading.

Self-Test. A self-test is a series of questions, exercises, or other means of measuring personal skill, knowledge, attitudes, or other aspects of behavior. The self-testing instrument or device may be student or teacher constructed or in some instances standardized, but in each case administered by and to the individual personally. Sometimes the student competes against his previous record, as in certain physical education activities, or against norms established individually, for the class, or even nationally.

Chapter 5

Teacher Initiated Techniques and Procedures

I shall light a candle of understanding in thine heart, which shall not be put out.

The Apocrypha

To be effective, good teaching demands careful preparation, planning, and implementation, requiring not only a thorough knowledge of a given subject field, but also applied imagination and functional anticipation. Effective teaching is in actuality the culmination of a series of preparatory activities which set the stage for learning.

Unexpected situations frequently occur in the classroom that demand teacher judgment and skill. No degree of planning and preparation can possibly anticipate every conceivable circumstance. Yet the overall process of directing learning is enhanced by strategical planning. Systematic attention to the methods and procedures which are largely teacher initiated is a vital element in the instructional situation.

Meaning of Teacher Initiated Procedures. Many types of instructional methods produce high-quality learning when properly applied. In all instances the teacher has a fundamental role as the director of learning activities. Some procedures of instruction, however, place a greater emphasis upon the teacher as the initiating force. These techniques have been identified in this chapter as "teacher initiated procedures."

Values of Information-Giving Procedures. The "telling" techniques of teaching have seen a very definite decline in recent years, although all educators recognize the importance of "informing" in the learning process. Hoover indicated some of the benefits of certain information-giving procedures. With specific reference to lecturing, demonstrations, and reporting, he proposed the following advantages:

> This method of gathering facts is economical of time and materials.
>
> It serves to channel the thinking of all students in a given direction.
>
> The approach enables the instructor to correct misunderstandings, or otherwise baffling situations, almost immediately.
>
> Demonstrations, especially, enable the class leader to utilize activities which would be too dangerous for the pupils themselves to perform within the ordinary classroom.
>
> Informal lectures, and to some extent reports and demonstrations, are easy to prepare, as they are usually based on specialized knowledge of the leader.[1]

Principles of Organization and Approach. Good planning and organization are fundamental to the teaching-learning situation. Probably more instructional uncertainty or outright failure is due to a lack of sound organization than to any other single reason. The following broad organizational guides concerning the use of teacher initiated techniques and procedures are useful in planning classroom activities. Organization should:

> Consider if there is anything so fundamental that it must precede, come at the outset, be included early.
>
> Contribute to focus and impact.
>
> Consider what provides the most inclusive and manageable overview.

---

[1] Kenneth H. Hoover, *Learning and Teaching in the Secondary School* (Boston: Allyn and Bacon, Inc., 1964), pp. 374-75.

Contribute to retention and transfer.

Consider what coverage should or might be anticipated and at what rate.

Consider what steps seem most logical and likely to move us forward toward our goals.[2]

General Principles Related to Study Activities. A good teacher is never completely satisfied with his techniques and methods of instruction. "The best teacher," according to Hoover, "is always in the process of 'becoming'." The following principles, selected from a more comprehensive list, are proposed as a useful framework for guiding the learning process:

> The key factor in the direction of study activities is the assignment . . . As an integral part of the classroom experience, they are made whenever class activities clearly indicate their need. There is no best time for making an assignment. . . Assignments which are cooperatively given are frequently cooperatively completed, involving student teams and committees. . . Class and/or school study are useful in providing needed direction in the early phases of assignment activities. Guided class study provides opportunities for diagnostic and remedial work associated with study activities. . . Whenever possible, assignments must foster creativity and originality. The ultimate end of study activities is to prepare the student to direct his own learning.[3]

Current Events

Current events are concerned with immediate or recent happenings which may be expressed through various means of communication. They include important circumstances as reported through newspapers, periodicals, popular magazines, radio, television, interviews, or other informative sources. Current events serve as a medium for relating local, state, national, or global occurrences to an understanding of everyday life.

---

[2] Joseph Leese, Kenneth Frasure, and Mauritz Johnson, Jr., *The Teacher in Curriculum Making* (New York: Harper & Row, Publishers, 1961), pp. 178-81.

[3] Hoover, *op. cit.*, pp. 508-09.

Procedural Steps

Selection of topic: Student participation might be enlisted in deciding upon a current theme. The topic should be consistent with the objectives of the planned program but could arise from a significant event itself. Certain areas lend themselves more appropriately to the approach than others.

Organization: Introduce the topic or topics. Identify the purposes. Divide the class into groups if different topics or phases of the same topic are to be investigated. Independent work by each student should be encouraged whether done in groups or as an individual project. Establish deadline dates for the reporting of events.

Collection of materials: Encourage the widespread use of all available sources of information on the subject, providing examples and giving illustrations of what is to be included. Individuals should be given some latitude in investigating different aspects which might be of interest. Discuss the process of selection and use of materials.

Checking the information: Insure that information and materials are up-to-date, significant, appropriate, and relevant to the topic. Organize the materials in a logical fashion. Provide for an understanding of the process of collection as well as the information presented. Allow some class time for the discussion and synthesis of ideas and information.

Presentation: The presenting of current events may be accomplished as a major project or done daily as an on-going activity of the group. Both oral and written reports might be utilized. Allow adequate time for questions and open discussion. Offer suggestions, constructive criticism, and additional information. Discuss the sources of data, the value of the information, and the implications of the material.

Application: Relate the material to class work which is in progress. Utilize maps, globes, charts, bulletin boards, and other aids to supplement the information and increase understanding. Follow up with appropriate individual and group projects. Relate the material to new and developing activities.

Advantages and Values

Current events:

Increase the power of discrimination, comprehension, critical analysis, and thinking and are rich in potential opportunities for concomitant learning.

Can be easily obtained, compiled, and consolidated individually or in groups and develop skills in locating and reporting.

Acquaint students with a variety of reliable sources of up-to-date information and with basic criteria by which they might be evaluated.

Increase understandings of and appreciations for happenings in civic affairs, daily life, and the everyday world.

Limitations and Problems

The use of current events requires a strong background, thorough understanding, and up-to-date preparedness by the teacher.

An understanding and appreciation of the past may be neglected if current events are over-emphasized or too frequently used as a basis for instruction.

Some students, in certain instances, may not have access to current literature and recommended media and some content areas are not as appropriate as others for utilizing the approach.

Current events are frequently reported in a sensational fashion which may lead to misunderstanding or distortion of facts.

Examples

Printed materials, especially newspapers, are primary sources of current event information. These are supplemented with information obtained via radio, television, and other communications media. All play an important part in helping to make local, national, and world events come to life in the classroom.

An interesting application of the current event was that conceived in an Illinois social studies class by Haner. He reported the characteristics of the unique approach as follows:

> As students enter the social-studies classroom, they are greeted by the colorful "Wall of the World." In the center of the wall is a large red-white-and-blue design showing a great compass superimposed upon a circular map of one hemisphere. Around this circle, at the four points of the compass, are the usual letters indicating the direction, but the E for East and the W for West are repeated in a vertical column between the N and the S so that the column spells out N-E-W-S and suggests the origin of news at the "four corners" of the world.
>
> The space . . . is filled with posters and news material . . . Colorful maps, newspaper headlines, news items, feature stories, and illustrations . . . Sprinkled all through these materials, as a special seasoning, are news cartoons . . . The space on the right of the compass is reserved for the students' own contributions and it is replete with materials . . . They bring the world into the classroom and hang it on the wall, and after that it becomes increasingly their world.[4]

Demonstration

The demonstration is a process of graphic explanation of a selected idea, fact, relationship, or phenomenon. It involves the use of materials and provides a visual experience which is usually increased in value by verbal explanation. The demonstration generally is utilized with a group of observer-participants by someone who is an expert on the given subject. It often is used to set a goal of activity or to define standards of performance. It centers attention upon processes, relationships, or reactions which result from a skilled manipulation of objects, machines, or appliances.

Procedural Steps

Selection of idea: Identify the content to be included in the demonstration. Establish some basic objectives which relate to the unit under study. Investigate different demonstration approaches

---

[4] Wendell Haner, "The Wall of the World," *Clearing House,* 23:92-93, Oct., 1948.

which might be used. Insure that adequate and appropriate equipment and materials are available and accessible.

Preparation: Decide upon the demonstration to be used and the procedures to be followed. Outline the key points to be demonstrated and discussed. Clearly understand the entire procedure. Obtain the necessary equipment and materials to be utilized.

Rehearsal: Set up the necessary apparatus and test each piece of equipment carefully. Conduct each step of the demonstration as planned. Make any pertinent changes and improvements. Anticipate any student questions which might arise during the demonstration. Prepare detailed notes on the procedures to be followed.

Introduction: Clearly explain the purpose and general outcomes of the demonstration. It is usually used to emphasize something which has already been discussed, to illustrate a specific point, to show how something is effectively done, or to facilitate learning in a specific prearranged sequence. Arrange the seating to insure a clear view by all students. Indicate the relationship of the demonstration to previously completed work. Remove all distractions.

Presentation: Keep the demonstration simple and as brief as possible. Insure that all equipment and materials are operable and arranged in proper order of presentation. Support the demonstration with pictures, charts, and other supplementary materials to aid comprehension. Check continuously to insure clear understanding by all students. Do not prolong or hurry the demonstration. Allow time for students to record important data and to ask questions. Summarize the information presented as the demonstration proceeds. Use objects and materials that are large enough to be observed and used easily. Do not divert from the main ideas. Direct student attention to the significant facts and relationships.

Discussion: Allow sufficient time for discussion during and following the demonstration. Attempt to answer all questions regarding aspects of the demonstration which were not clearly understood. Repeat certain phases of the demonstration, if desirable and feasible. Raise further questions and identify related problems for study. Stimulate and guide students critically to analyze, compare, contrast, and evaluate the results. Encourage student generalizations, inferences, and summarization. Note possible improvements for later use. Carefully dismantle and store the equipment and materials for future utilization.

Advantages and Values

Demonstration:

Creates a high degree of attention, concentration, and interest which can be further exploited by other techniques and further study.

Can be performed by the teacher or the student and is particularly valuable in learning specific skills.

Provides a concrete and realistic visual picture of what is being presented to supplement word images and usually results in a more lasting impression.

Is less time consuming than individual experimentation and can be used with large or small groups of any age under controlled conditions.

Can be repeated in part or in total, slowed down or speeded up, and easily adapted or adjusted to the age group and a desirable pace for learning.

Limitations and Problems

The demonstration requires careful planning, detailed preparation, and considerable skill to be effective.

Without proper direction and guidance, students may concentrate upon the aids used and ignore the lesson itself.

The necessary equipment, special supplies, and materials needed for the demonstration may be expensive, difficult to obtain, and hard to handle and store.

The demonstration is best adapted to certain subject fields, such as natural science, and cannot be easily used by all teachers.

Certain complications may arise during the demonstration, such as poorly functioning equipment, breakage, or unpredictable results.

Examples

Demonstrations have great value as an instructional method to demonstrate ideas, skills, processes, and other phenomena. Several simplified illustrations might include demonstrating light transmission, breathing or respiration, making candy or bread, tying a knot, using a slide rule, disinfecting a wound, and driving an automobile.

A demonstration might be used in illustrating the nature, transmission, and reproduction of microorganisms:

> To begin, sterilize several glass containers and lids in boiling water. Agar plates are best but if they are not available baby food jars can be used. Combine and pour a mixture of gelatin and bouillon into the bottom of the containers, about a half inch thick. Cover the containers with the lids and allow the solution to harden. Next, open the containers and smear each hardened portion of the material with a different substance, such as saliva from the mouth, a touch with a dirty finger, some dust from the floor, or a swab from the teeth. Be sure to label each container carefully. Place the containers in a warm and dark place. It should be possible every few days to observe the growth of the materials. A microscope or magnifying glass is useful in observation in the early stages of growth. Discussion might be focused on ideas related to the nature of the growth process, how microorganisms reproduce under different conditions, and how transmission can occur by direct contact.

Field Trip

The field trip, sometimes called the excursion, is a visit to some location other than the normal classroom for educational purposes. Confirmatory field trips serve as a reinforcement for previously acquired learning while the exploratory excursion fulfills the basic function of discovery. Each approach is a structured attempt to provide an on-the-spot observation of some specific process, undertaking, or activity.

Procedural Steps

Identification of the unit of study: Insure that the topic selected is appropriate for field trip observation. The excursion should be the best approach as a learning experience and satisfy established objectives for the unit.

Planning: Good preliminary planning is the most vital factor for a successful field trip. Some student participation might be solicited in determining the place to visit. Select several possible locations to be visited. Make the necessary arrangements with the personnel involved. Check all details of facilities, time, and other considerations. Work out the question of what is to be observed with the sponsoring organization. Develop a definite time schedule including departure, observation, and return. Visit the establishment beforehand, if possible.

Administrative and organizational details: Obtain the permission of the school administration to take the field trip. Distribute and receive parental permission slips from each participating student. Provide for suitable transportation if required. Make provisions for eating whenever necessary.

Preparation: Generally outline and discuss what to look for during the field trip. Indicate any special clothing to be worn or materials to be included on the excursion. Caution the class with respect to any safety precautions or general rules and regulations which should be followed. As a group, identify some possible questions that might arise.

Conducting the field trip: Insure that there is adequate supervision provided. Keep a close watch on the movements of the group to avoid straying or misconduct. Be prepared to answer questions as they arise or to enlist the assistance of the individual in charge of the visit. Provide for a certain amount of student freedom during the excursion insofar as is feasible.

Discussion: Arrange for letters of appreciation to be sent to the sponsoring individuals or organization. Enlist student participation in this courtesy. Facilitate a meaningful discussion of the experience. Outline the main ideas and summarize the observations. Develop other student activities as an outgrowth of the excursion. Allow students to assist in an appraisal of the field trip.

Advantages and Values

The field trip:

Helps to bridge the gap between the school and the community and the gulf which often exists between different subjects in the curriculum.

Develops self-activity in learning and self-reliance in assessing situations and solving problems.

Affords valuable opportunities to foster vocational and educational guidance by providing some explanation and understanding of a range of occupations or professions.

Provides a social type contact between the teacher and students which may favorably enhance future class relations.

Affords opportunities for exploration, investigation, and discovery in real life situations which amplify and extend theoretical study.

Limitations and Problems

Field trips may become extremely time consuming and costly and must be continually evaluated in light of educational values.

A lack of careful attention to the many essential details of planning and preparation can result in embarrassing situations and serious legal problems.

Special excursions as a reward for good behavior and trips which are not an integral part of the planned educational program should be subjected to close examination.

Unforeseen emergencies, distractions, and a variety of other personal and group problems are likely to arise and should be anticipated and controlled insofar as possible.

Examples

Almost unlimited possibilities exist for planned visits outside the regular classroom. Excursions might be developed to such interesting places as: a factory, water purification plant, museum, soil-conservation project, bakery, weather station, dairy, zoo, fire station, television studio, newspaper office, or department store.

An overnight field trip to selected schools using educational radio was reported by Dale. Although more elaborate than most normal excursions, the experience described by Geraldine McMullin, a Rochester, New York teacher, provides some excellent operational guidelines for the activity:

> Arrangements were made in advance so that hotel reservations were verified; easy-to-follow maps were drawn for locating the hotel. And there had been enough discussion in the groups so that the participants knew what to look for in the classes which were to be observed. And good ground work had been

laid for the trip, the purpose of which was to observe the actual use of radio in the classroom.

The staff of the radio station had also done an excellent job of preparing for their visitors. An outline of our complete visit was given to us, with schools, programs, teachers, and principals listed. Observations and discussions were scheduled so that no time was lost in trying to locate schools or grades that were listening to programs.

Representatives of the staff explained the purposes, functions, and content of the broadcasts for elementary, junior-high, and high-school groups. After all observations had been completed, provision was made for discussion with the staff and various supervisors. This was good follow-through because it allowed for questions, suggestions, and criticisms, all of which were most enlightening. The personnel were open-minded and ready to accept new ideas and concrete suggestions.[5]

Other Teacher Initiated Procedures

Anecdotal record. The anecdotal record is a descriptive account of events, episodes, or circumstances in the daily school life of the student that preserves significant incidents and information concerning actual student behavior for subsequent review. As such, it is an aid to help the teacher determine most effective instructional procedures. The major purpose of the anecdotal record is to provide a clear perspective and reference to certain kinds of student behavior through systematic observation and evaluation.

Conference. A conference is a meeting of individuals for the purpose of presenting information, finding answers to questions, discovering solutions to problems, or of adjusting differences of opinion. It is the pooling of the knowledge and experience of individuals through consultation and discussion of common problems or interests. The conference may be composed of only several persons or a large number. All conferences, however, are organized with a definite purpose or objective. Conferences also involve discussion through which decisions can be made.

---

[5] Edgar Dale, *Audio-Visual Methods in Teaching*, rev. ed. (New York: The Dryden Press, 1954), pp. 170-71. Used by permission of Holt, Rinehart and Winston, Inc., present publisher, and the author.

Counseling. Counseling consists of individualized and personalized assistance, advice, or deliberation designed to help the student make adjustments or achieve that which he is capable of accomplishing. In use by the teacher, counseling usually is conducted through personal interview in which the student is aided to make certain choices or decisions. Various specialized counselors, such as remedial, psychological, vocational, and placement counselors, are sometimes employed by the school to provide individualized assistance.

Drill. Drill consists of the systematic and repetitive practice of certain fundamental skills to help bring about automatic response, accuracy, perfection, or speed of performance. It can be used for the corrective purpose of eliminating errors, for overcoming hesitancy or uncertainty, or for widening the span of recognition. Although applicable to most subjects, it especially is useful in formal handwriting, physical education, music, typewriting, rhythmic activities, mathematics, and similar fields of study.

Guidance. Guidance is a form of systematic assistance to help students assess their abilities, capabilities, and limitations in order that they might learn more effectively. The approach involves a dynamic interpersonal relationship designed to influence the ultimate behavior of the individual. It can be carried out individually or in groups.

Indoctrination. Indoctrination literally means to imbue with learning, principles, or doctrines. It is a means of introducing ready-made opinions or proved ideas to the student without great concern for the reasoning process. Persuasion is the basic approach.

Interview. An interview is a face-to-face procedure designed to elicit information outside the classroom which is related to current study. Interviews of appropriate individuals frequently are conducted by a single student or in groups of not more than three students and reported back to the class in summary form. Teachers also use the interview technique with students and parents.

Lecture. The lecture method involves the formalized presentation of information by the teacher through oral exposition. It generally utilizes certain essential facts or basic information to impart knowledge, create interest, influence opinion, stimulate activity, or promote critical thinking. The lecture technique emphasizes oral expression but frequently is supplemented by any number of related teaching aids or instructional materials. It proceeds with a minimum of class participation and interruption.

Lecture-Discussion. The lecture-discussion incorporates the desirable qualities of both the lecture and discussion into a formal technique. It consists of a verbal form of presentation with provision for clarification and further enlightenment through class participation and intergroup exchange.

Outside Speaker. The outside speaker, sometimes referred to as a resource person or guest speaker, is an individual who is invited to talk to a group on a given topic or subject. The person usually is selected because of some special knowledge, talent, or experience which classifies him as an expert or an authority in the particular field.

Question and Answer. The question and answer technique ordinarily is developed in a discussion-type setting. It may be carried out by the class under teacher or student direction or used in conjunction with resource persons. It especially is valuable to project the combined knowledge of the group relating to new or technical information. The question and answer approach frequently is involved as a part of other learning procedures.

Review. Review entails the re-examination or re-evaluation of material previously presented or studied. It involves an overview of a unit of work or body of material in an attempt to identify the most important ideas and concepts. The review represents a guided effort which facilitates clarity of understanding and the formulation of final generalizations. A variety of related techniques is commonly used in the review session.

Test. A test, commonly called an examination or quiz, is a device or procedure used to measure ability, achievement, attitude, interest, understanding, or some other aspect of behavior. It may be objective or subjective in its measurement. There are numerous types of tests, such as those designed to indicate aptitude, appreciation, comprehension, character, cooperation, deduction, intelligence, knowledge, and personality. The teacher ordinarily is concerned with oral or written tests incorporating questions of an essay, multiple-choice, matching, association, true-false, identification, missing-parts, completion, short answer, or problem solving nature.

Chapter 6

Material Focused Techniques and Procedures

Seeing much, suffering much and studying much are the three pillars of learning.

Benjamin Disraeli

Teaching materials are an essential part of an effective educational program. They provide a good substitute for first-hand experience, and, when properly used, do much to foster learning. Through their varying appeals, instructional materials are an important asset in extending and enriching the curriculum at all educational levels.

Meaning of Material Focused Procedures. A variety of terms has been applied to indicate the involvement of the several senses in the learning process. Supplementary materials, audio-visual aids, multi-sensory materials, perceptual aids to learning, and instructional materials are phrases frequently used in connection with the audio-visual field. Supplementary materials help to "put across" the substance of instruction. How these materials are used become the techniques and procedures of education.

Values of Material Focused Procedures. Instructional materials that are well planned and used in the classroom are significant adjuncts to meaningful learning experiences. They assist in encouraging students to find answers to problems, to discover, and to extend understandings.

Certain specific and practical values of perceptual materials were outlined by Kinder. He identified and discussed the following contributions of materials to instruction. They:

> Overcome the limitations of restricted personal experiences of pupils; Overcome the limitations of the classroom; Provide for the direct interaction of the pupils with the realities of the social and physical environment; Provide uniformity of percepts; Give initial concepts which are correct, real, and complete; Awaken new desires and interests; Provide motivation and stimulation; and, Provide integrated experiences which vary from concrete to abstract.[1]

Principles of Effective Material Focused Activities. The vast range of materials and resources available for instruction make their selection and use one of the critical decisions in good teaching. Questions such as the following provide guidelines for the evaluation of materials to be included in the classroom for a particular group of students:

> Does the material relate and contribute to the content structure of the curriculum?
>
> Will the use of the material strengthen pupil skills in understanding, critical thinking, problem solving, and ability to communicate?
>
> Will the material contribute to attitudes and deepen appreciations?
>
> Are materials sufficiently varied to meet the range of abilities, needs, interests, and maturity levels of the individual pupils?
>
> Are the materials adequate for the number of children in the classroom?
>
> Are materials arranged and organized to provide for the maximum utilization of space, easy access, and ready availability?[2]

---

[1] James E. Kinder, *Audio-Visual Materials and Techniques* (New York: American Book Co., 1959), pp. 42-45.

[2] Lois Knox, Margaret Lenz, and Thelma Beardsley, *The Use of Contemporary Materials in the Classroom,* Department of Elementary-Kindergarten-Nursery Education (Washington: National Education Association, 1963), p. 3.

Knox, Lenz, and Beardsley raised several important questions with respect to the use of instructional materials in the classroom. They identified perhaps the single most significant factor—the teacher—in the use of resources in instruction:

> Contemporary materials available to both teacher and pupil potentially make the classroom a rich laboratory for learning, a stimulating and challenging place for working. The fulfillment of this potential depends on the way in which the available materials are used. The question, "What materials are provided in the classroom?" is indeed important, but its value is dependent on a second question, "How does the teacher utilize these materials in attaining educational goals?" An answer to the first is meaningless without an answer to the second. The school assumes much of the responsibility for the provision of materials, but the teacher alone determines the effectiveness of such materials by the way in which he utilizes them.[3]

Bulletin Board

The bulletin board is a sheet of wood, masonite, cork, celotex, or similar material usually set within a frame. It sometimes is called a tackboard or pinning board and may be used for displaying pictures, charts, posters, clippings, examples of student work, photographs, or other learning materials. The bulletin board offers infinite possibilities for presenting visual material. It may be used in the classroom, corridor, library, gymnasium, office, cafeteria, study hall, auditorium, and other locations.

Procedural Steps

Obtaining the bulletin board: Decide upon where the bulletin board is to be located. A portable-type board may be desirable since it can be utilized in multiple ways and under varying circumstances. Recognize the purpose of the bulletin board and different ways in which it might be used effectively.

Selection of topic: The display materials should be appropriate

---

[3] *Ibid.*, p. 28.

for the particular lesson and adaptable to the age group in question. The subject should lend itself to the display technique. Usually the basic topic or subject should be apparent at a glance.

Selection of caption or main theme: A slogan, popular phrase, question, or another attention-getting theme should be used. Details on how best to present the idea should be considered. A good display must attract and hold attention.

Preparation: A variety of possibilities should be considered such as pictures, silhouettes, pamphlets, small objects or specimens, photographs, cartoons, charts, and posters. Materials to be displayed should be mounted or backed with colorful and durable heavy paper. This adds to their appearance, artistic value, and stability for future use.

Arrangement: Care should be given to the unity and organization of the material. Avoid crowding by limiting the number of materials used and the amount of printed statements. Insure that all materials are firmly attached to the board. Select a few well mounted materials that suit the specific purpose and arrange them skillfully to put across the main idea. Directional arrows or heavy yarn might be used to help indicate relationships or to lead the viewers eye toward a desired section. One major idea or theme should be stressed. Decide on the purpose of the display. The bold and forceful use of color should be considered. The assistance of the art teacher might be enlisted as an artistic arrangement is essential to a good display.

Lettering and printed material: All printed material should be clear and legible. The captions should be directly related to the display material. Vocabulary should be appropriate to the grade level. The use of pins to produce a three dimensional effect, block-type letters, and other interesting approaches might be used. Words and sentences having a functional meaning might provide experience in spelling and reading.

Utilization: Place the display at eye level, if possible. Student participation in the development of the display and the mounting of objects might be encouraged. The display might be compiled during class as well as prior to a given lesson. Emphasize the major theme, show important relationships to subject matter, and encourage questions and responses concerning the material.

Evaluation: The bulletin board should be appraised in terms of its artistic and technical appearance, consistency, interest, and educational value. Any appropriate changes or improvements should be noted. Encourage students to observe and use the information presented on the board. Students might be involved in the planning, preparation, compilation, and evaluation of the display.

Rotation of material: Remove the particular display once it has served its purpose or as student interest wanes. Attempt to determine the effect of the material on learning. Enlist student help in selecting topics for future development and display. Storage of the materials as a unit will save much time and effort at a later date. The display might serve in the future to initiate a unit, culminate a lesson, for review, or as the central focus for a particular study session.

Advantages and Values

The bulletin board:

Provides a practical outlet for artistic talent and creative ability for both the teacher and the student.

May help to unify class spirit by creating a feeling of responsibility, appreciation, and accomplishment when developed by the group.

Stimulates considerable student interest and enthusiasm for a particular lesson when properly planned and developed.

Provides a permanent or movable place that is convenient for the display of all types of educational materials.

Limitations and Problems

The bulletin board display, by virtue of its nature, cannot involve highly complex ideas or concepts.

The materials on the bulletin board must be changed frequently or they may be taken for granted and lose their interest and value as a learning device.

To be effective, the bulletin board must be simple and telegraph its message quickly, easily, and efficiently.

There is a distinct tendency to "overload" the bulletin board rather than to concentrate on a single idea or main theme.

The better bulletin boards are relatively expensive, although teacher constructed boards are quite easy to make at a small cost.

Examples

Unlimited possibilities exist for effective bulletin board displays in connection with other teaching procedures. Materials can be collected and arranged for viewing following a field trip, as the result of research on a specific topic, or as a culminating activity for various class projects. The display might depict any number of themes, such as Travel through Time, The Olympic Games, Good Neighbors in Foreign Countries, Media of Communication, or Food Fads and Fallacies using such materials as cartoons, newspapers, book jackets, ribbons or colored strings, drawings, snapshots, posters, stick figures, and postcards. Displays also can be developed to illustrate local history, industrial achievements, medical discovery, hobbies or leisure time activities, famous people, foreign lands, or various products. Grubola described other themes related to conservation and some ideas for display construction:

> Themes for displays might include: forest fires—their cost and prevention; how to stop erosion; the problem of the falling water table; flood control—why and how; conservation means wise use, not hoarding; how Americans have used their minerals; wild animals are resources too. Maps, drawings, graphs, and pictures may be combined to present facts, stir the imagination, and call for action on any of these themes. Younger children may use animal pictures (which create a good deal of interest) to show what can happen to animals in the forests during a long, cold winter.[4]

Exhibit

The exhibit is a display of materials which has as its purpose informing the observer about a subject of educational significance. It usually provides a realistic impression through the use of three-dimensional objects rather than flat materials, and frequently makes use of sound, color, and motion. An exhibit may include posters, pictures, charts, graphs, specimens, and other similar

---

[4] Marion R. Grubola, *How to Use a Bulletin Board*, rev. ed., How to Do It Series, No. 4 (Washington: National Council for the Social Studies, 1965), pp. 2-3.

materials. It also may incorporate recordings, films, slides, and other audio or visual materials.

Procedural Steps

Establishing the content: Decide on the subject matter or main ideas to be displayed by use of the exhibit. Identify the purpose and the expected values of the exhibit.

Developing a plan: An exhibit may be constructed by the teacher or the students or may be obtained on loan from numerous commercial groups, museums, and other organizations devoted to civic or educational purposes. Keep in mind that the exhibit intimately involves the viewer. Plan for the materials which might be used and the major concepts to be emphasized. Consider the overall layout carefully.

Principles: A single main idea or theme should be emphasized. The effectiveness of the exhibit is increased if objects can be easily observed, understood, touched, and manipulated. Motion, color, and sound help to attract attention and should be used whenever possible. Keep the exhibit as simple as possible while still getting across the message. An exhibit is to be seen and not read. Keep the labels and printed information short, legible, and to the point.

Construction: Follow the fundamental principles of good exhibit planning and construction in the development of the display. Rearrange the materials to provide for the greatest possible impact on the observer. Avoid overloading the exhibit with too many materials or too much printed matter. Consider the available space for the exhibit before beginning its construction.

Utilization: Place the exhibit in a conspicuous and well lighted location. Arrange for its use in relation to the unit under study. Encourage student comments and discussion concerning the exhibit and its relation to the lesson. Once it has served its purpose, arrange for dismantling the exhibit and storing it for future use.

Advantages and Values

The exhibit:

Provides an ideal opportunity for the encouragement of student creativity, originality, and manipulative skill.

Facilitates the understanding of complex processes, difficult relationships, and the application of concepts to concrete situations.

Has good value as a testing device by involving the labeling of different parts, the naming of specific items, or the comprehension of concepts.

Can sometimes improve upon reality by accentuating important features and simplifying more complicated aspects, such as may be found in cutaway models which provide interior views or objects with movable parts.

Limitations and Problems

Many of the most effective exhibits involve combinations of motion, color, and sound and are quite expensive to purchase or construct.

Adequate and appropriate space for both display and storage of an exhibit can be a problem.

The functional use of an exhibit is frequently destroyed if a part is lost, misplaced, damaged, or broken.

Planning and preparing a good exhibit can be extremely time consuming and requires a good degree of artistic ability and mechanical knowledge.

Some supervision and explanation of an exhibit is often necessary to prevent indiscriminate use and improper handling of the materials.

Examples

An illustration of one functional exhibit was provided by East:

> Perhaps your students are interested in making bread. An exhibit can show some of the steps in the process and something of the action of the yeast. The measured ingredients and the equipment are placed together. Then glass bowls of dough in various stages of rising are placed in proper sequence. Finally a shaped loaf rising and a baked loaf complete the display. By simple explanatory labels the whole process is made understandable. The yeast really acts, and the dough really rises, and the students can't help learning.[5]

---

[5] Marjorie East, *Display for Learning* (New York: Holt, Rinehart and Winston, Inc., 1952), p. 32.

Flannel Board

A flannel or felt board is simply a piece of heavy cardboard, ply-wood, or other stiff material tightly covered with flannel or felt cloth. Objects treated with a sensitive backing may be attached to this surface. The board may be purchased or constructed in a variety of sizes and shapes and utilized for instruction in many different ways. The materials to be displayed on the board may be backed with sandpaper, blotter material, felt, flocked paper, styro-foam, flannel, or a similar substance.

Procedural Steps

Selection of topic: The subject should be related to the unit of work under study and adapted to the age group that will view it. The use of the flannel board as the best possible technique for the lesson in question should be considered. Adequate materials should be readily accessible for the board.

Construction: Inexpensive flannel boards are available for pur-chase or materials can easily be obtained to construct one. If con-structing a board, stretch the material tight over the board and tack or tape it on the opposite side or on the ends. Some boards may be slip-covered to permit use of both sides. Two boards constructed separately and then hinged together will provide a large board that can be folded to facilitate handling and to conserve storage space. The board should be light in weight, yet durable. It should be easy to manipulate. The cover material for the board may be obtained in a variety of different colors to suit individual taste.

Development: Encourage student participation in the collection and preparation of visual materials to be used with the board. Select materials that are large enough to be observed easily, yet small enough to fit the available space. Insure that the size propor-tions of the materials are approximate to prevent false impressions or perceptions. Cut out the material, paste it on heavy paper or light cardboard, and strip the back with a sensitized substance, such as coarse sandpaper, which will adhere firmly to the board.

Planning: Assemble all the materials which have been prepared for the lesson. Arrange the items in a logical sequence. Eliminate those that do not contribute to the lesson and its predetermined objectives. Practice the presentation, following a prepared outline. Continuously check the layout for proper spacing and effect. Check the eye appeal and color contrast. Prepare and view the use of all printed materials. Anticipate and note any problems that might likely arise and ways of dealing with them.

Introduction: Orient the class to the general topic and the use of the flannel board, if necessary or desirable. Lead into the use of the board skillfully, not abruptly. Clearly identify student responsibilities such as note taking and any active participation in the lesson.

Utilization: Place the board at eye level, if possible, and at a slightly backward incline. Use a minimum of objects at any one time to emphasize a central idea. Take advantage of student participation and opportunities for incidental learning. Encourage students to identify and handle objects and discuss information related to the lesson.

Discussion: Show the relevance and usefulness of the information covered to the unit of study. Note any ways in which the lesson might be changed or improved for future presentation. When completed, store together the materials used for future use.

Advantages and Values

The flannel board:

Provides for a simple and rapid manipulation, reproduction, and organization of concrete information and related materials.

Is relatively durable and lasting and can be adapted to a variety of uses for almost all subject matter fields.

May be utilized to tell a story, present a skill, illustrate a concept, or show a relationship in a sequential piece-by-piece manner.

May be used by students as well as the teacher in presenting information, giving demonstrations and reports, and developing other creative activities.

Limitations and Problems

Unless properly constructed and used, materials easily may be blown off the board, knocked down, or otherwise disturbed.

Some flannel boards are too large, bulky, or heavy and difficult to handle or store easily.

A good amount of time is required to collect and prepare display items, plan a lesson, and skillfully use the flannel board.

The flannel board is not effective for extremely large groups because of the difficulty in viewing.

Examples

The flannel or felt board is an extremely adaptable device for use in many subjects and at all grade levels. The broad application of the technique at specific grades, for varying purposes, and by different individuals was well expressed by Stoops who stated:

> On the elementary level some of the common uses of the flannel board are for color recognition, number combinations, reading readiness, storytelling, word recognition, dramatization, reading music, map work, composition in art, and relationships of fractions.
>
> On junior and senior high school levels the flannel board can be used just as widely for such things as foreign language vocabulary and grammar drills, weather maps, political and economic maps, diagrams for game plays and dance steps, floor plans for furniture arrangement, scale layouts for planning large areas such as gardens or whole farms, plans for engineering drawings, and maps and recognition drills for driver training.[6]

Other Material Focused Procedures

Calendar. The calendar is a visual aid which indicates the month and date and provides space in which to enter selected information. It is a device which can be used effectively to stimulate interest in a given subject or circumstance. Historically significant events as well as current happenings can be considered.

Cartoon. The cartoon is a form of comic art which can be used in education to depict important events, personalities, or circumstances. It presents a simulated but usually easily recognized and popular graphic illustration of selected activity or behavior.

Chart. The chart consists of visual symbols which may be used to summarize, contrast, compare, or explain subject matter. Charts

---

[6] Betty Stoops, "Facts and Fun on Flannel Board," *Educational Screen, 31*: 324-25, Oct., 1952.

reflect a wide range of interests and are commonly referred to by type, such as narrative, skill development, creative expression, reference, experience, teacher composed, informational, or guidance charts. They represent one of the oldest forms of teaching.

Graph. Graphs involve various levels of visual expression ranging from a simple presentation of information to the most abstract statistical analysis. Graphic presentation serves the major functions of providing a concise summary, indicating a comparison, showing a relationship, or otherwise explaining a concept or idea.

Map. A map, according to Webster, is a representation, usually on a flat surface, of the face of the earth or some part of it. It shows relative size and position according to a scale, projection, or represented position. Various types of maps can be used in the classroom, such as contour, relief, dot, crosshatch, and pin maps. Maps also can be used to illustrate physical, political, social, commercial, or economic dimensions.

Mobile. A mobile is a set or series of objects which are delicately balanced and suspended from a central point on string, fine wire, or thread in such a way as to sway with air movements. It commonly is constructed in a counterbalanced multiple form which rotates within itself and as a total assembly.

Model. The model is a recognizable three-dimensional imitation or replica of a real object. It usually is identical to the original in most respects except size and incorporates the essential features of the object or procedure.

Mock-up. The mock-up is an instructional device that approximates a scale model of a real object or a part of the object. It alters the elements of the original object, often simplifying or exaggerating details, to concentrate only on certain aspects in order to make them more teachable. Mock-ups commonly are used to help understand complex processes, such as engines or certain functions of the human body.

Pamphlets. A pamphlet is a paperbound document, usually consisting of a limited number of pages, which is ordinarily devoted to a particular subject. The content often is quite restricted in scope and covers a given subject in a somewhat general manner. Many free and inexpensive pamphlets are available for instructional use.

Pictures. Pictures are flat illustrative materials with little or no printed matter which are used to provide a visual experience. They can be utilized in a variety of ways, such as displayed on bulletin boards, projected, or organized in booklet form. Pictures frequently are used to translate word symbols, enrich reading experiences, correct mistaken impressions, motivate activity, or stir the imagination.

Poster. A poster is a pictorial or symbolic visual representation designed to catch and hold the observer's attention long enough to implant a significant message or idea. It is intended to convey a single easily grasped idea in an emphatic fashion. It stresses bold design, forceful color, clear organization, and careful word selection. It may vary from a simple printed card to highly artistic pictures and slogans. The use of the poster is many centuries old, having been utilized by early traders and merchants to advertise their wares.

Chapter 7

Equipment Centered Techniques and Procedures

Let him be kept from paper, pen, and ink;
So may he cease to write and learn to think.

Matthew Prior

Great strides have been made in recent years in the development of visual and auditory aids for learning. Advances, particularly in photography and electronics, have made it possible to create and utilize a variety of new teaching aids. Instructional techniques and procedures that involve various types of equipment help to bring sound, picture, and color into the modern classroom. Techniques which involve the use of equipment are appropriately called "equipment centered."

Values of Equipment Centered Techniques. Instruction utilizing audiovisual equipment is a potent contributing factor to better learning. Although there is no magical formula for teaching success, the use of the many available instructional devices and machines enable the student to learn more quickly and effectively. It has been pointed out that such instructional aids render service by:

Creating more vivid impressions; Using additional organs of sense; Getting and holding the student's attention through "change of pace"; Simplifying the knowledge to be learned; and, Improving the quality of the instruction given.[1]

It is apparent that the proper use of instructional materials and equipment contributes to effective learning in many ways. Hoover indicated seven general advantages as follows:

Instructional devices: (1) Reduce verbalism, (2) Increase the performance of learning, (3) Add interest and involvement, (4) Stimulate self-activity, (5) Provide a uniformity of percepts, (6) Provide continuity of thought, and (7) Provide experiences not easily obtained through other means.[2]

Advantages of Projected Aids. Much of the modern equipment available for instructional purposes makes use of the projection mechanism. Certain benefits of projected aids in particular were identified by DeBernardis. He suggested the following advantages:

Group instruction. Every teacher has found that a small picture or chart is difficult to use for a group presentation. Projection can make the picture large enough for all to see.

Centering attention. With a darkened room and a brilliant screen, it is easy to concentrate the attention of the class on the material being presented.

Creating interest. Projected pictures in themselves create a certain amount of interest. If not overused, the projected image can hold the attention of students on all levels.[3]

Chalkboard

The chalkboard is a smooth surface usually fastened to the wall or enclosed in a type of frame which is used to print, write, or draw upon with chalk. By contrast with the slate "blackboard" of former years, the modern chalkboard may be found in green, grey, blue,

---

[1] Kenneth B. Haas and Harry Q. Packer, *Preparation and Use of Audio-Visual Aids,* 3rd ed. (Englewood Cliffs, N.J.: Prentice-Hall, Inc., 1960), pp. 278-79.

[2] Kenneth H. Hoover, *Learning and Teaching in the Secondary School* (Boston: Allyn and Bacon, Inc., 1964), pp. 536-37.

[3] From: *The Use of Instructional Materials* by Amo DeBarnardis. Copyright © 1960, by Appleton-Century-Crofts, Inc. Reprinted by permission of Appleton-Century-Crofts.

or another pastel color. It is located in most classrooms as well as other instructional settings and it is constructed in varying sizes and shapes. As an accepted and integral part of teaching, the chalkboard is one of the oldest and most important forms of teaching aids.

Procedural Steps

Planning: Carefully consider what aspects of the lesson can best be shown through chalkboard use. It is well to practice writing, drawing, and printing on the board whenever possible. Consider chalkboard utilization by students as well as the teacher. Insure that the section of the board to be used is easily reached, especially when to be used by the student. Set up the details of the chalkboard plan on paper.

Materials: Obtain the necessary materials to be used with the presentation. Yellow chalk provides a generally better contrast than white chalk. Other colored chalk may be used for emphasis and clarity of any detailed work. Be sure that a clean eraser is available.

Selection of area: The space selected should be large enough to prevent the cramming of material. It should be easily visible to the entire class and as close to eye level as possible. The board should be free from glare and clear of other distracting materials.

Principles: Arrange the class to compensate for individual vision problems. Regulate the lighting where necessary. Print, write, or draw clearly and legibly. Avoid wordy descriptions and nonessentials. Use an eraser rather than a finger to correct errors. Stand comfortably to one side rather than in front of the work when using the board. Work in large patterns. Proceed rapidly during class time but not to the neglect of accuracy, neatness, and mechanical factors.

Development: Relate all chalkboard material to the lesson. The activity should be purposeful. If detailed in nature, board work should be completed prior to class in order to save instructional time. Proper principles of chalkboard work should be followed. The work should represent the teacher's or student's best effort. Encourage student participation where feasible.

Utilization: Apply the visual information to the lesson. Use diagrams, words, phrases, drawings and other techniques to clarify understandings and show relationships. Erase unrelated material as it is discussed and keep the board free from cluttering, but leave work on the board until all students have had ample time to copy or assimilate it.

Analyzation: Observe the effects of the approach. Record ideas for future use since an erasure loses the information forever. Step to the back of the room following class and appraise the material which was placed on the chalkboard during the lesson. Record ways in which the presentation might have been improved or changed.

Advantages and Values

The chalkboard:

Is a device which is readily available in most teaching situations, is relatively simple to use, and which can be used indefinitely without deterioration.

Facilitates the consistency of group work by providing exactly the same material or information to all class members.

May be used under certain conditions for a screen for projection purposes, map outlines, pictures, symbols, slides, fade outs, and other visual presentations.

Is useful for quickly presenting directions, outlines, summaries, or a synopsis of material covered or to be covered.

Limitations and Problems

The teacher must turn away from the group when using the chalkboard which hampers class contact and may result in classroom control problems.

Too frequently the chalkboard is used as a weak crutch in place of another technique that might be more effective and motivating.

Unless properly used, the chalkboard lacks the novelty that might be desired for attention and interest since it is an old stimulus.

Work left on the board from one class to another, chalk dust, partial erasures, and smeared boards are unsightly and may be distracting.

Unless properly located in a suitable environment, material presented on the chalkboard may be difficult to view by some class members, especially in a large group situation.

Examples

Among the most important items which can be presented via the chalkboard are daily problems, technical terms and definitions, drawings and sketches, outlines, announcements, diagrams, rules and policies, maps, graphs, directions, and reviews. Kinder spotlighted a number of considerations and factors related to chalkboard utilization along with certain values and limitations in using the technique. He pointed out that the teacher need not necessarily be an artist or a draftsman to make use of the chalkboard effectively. He suggested several helpful approaches—stick figure drawings, opaque projection, proportional squares, template method, and pattern method. With reference to specific fields of study, he offered the following useful hints:

> Other subjects which may make extensive use of the chalkboard and use permanent rulings or drawings are music, geography, and engineering. Rooms devoted to music can use a retained scoring of the staff and lines. In geography outline maps showing longitudinal and latitudinal lines are helpful. Classes in mathematics and engineering use cross-section rulings so often that a section of the chalkboard might well be arranged for this purpose.

> Filmstrips and lantern slides may be flashed on the chalkboard during reading lessons. Children may go to the board and underline or circle selected items with chalk. The image on the board is stable until the projector is shut off. Such a procedure provides variety and is easier than copying so many words, phrases, or sentences.[4]

Film

The film or motion picture is a sequence of photographs, pictures, or drawings which create an optical illusion of movement when projected on a screen in rapid succession. The motion picture encompasses visualization with or without color, music, narration,

---

[4] James S. Kinder, *Audio-Visual Materials and Techniques,* 2nd ed. (New York: American Book Co., 1959), p. 350.

or sound relationships. It is a method of transmitting stimuli and experiences by recreating events, situations, or circumstances through action.

Procedural Steps

Selection of film: Numerous film guide catalogs are available which assist in film selection. The film should be suited to the specific topic or problem under consideration, appropriate for the class, up-to-date, accurate, educationally sound, and should contribute authentic information of a high quality. Class or school produced films are now within the means of educational budgets and might be considered.

Preview: Study the film to ascertain its value in keeping with established needs and objectives for the lesson. It should be well organized and include fundamentally the information or impression desired. Read accompanying study guide if one is available. Carefully outline specific points and key ideas which should be emphasized in class.

Preparation of facilities and equipment: Some preparatory responsibilities might be handled by students. Set up the projector and screen. Wind the film and insure that it is ready for showing. Check the room temperature, ventilation, and lighting. Arrange the seating to insure a clear and unobstructed view for all students. Test the projector and establish the proper distance from the screen. Eliminate all unnecessary distractions.

Preparation of class: Preparation of the class might be done while the preceding arrangements are being accomplished. Indicate the purpose of the motion picture. Introduce the film and provide a brief general outline of content. Identify specific material which should receive more careful attention during the viewing.

Presentation: A student operator might be utilized to handle projection responsibilities. Be sure that the picture and sound are synchronized. Adjust the volume for easy hearing. Insure that the picture is focused and fits the screen properly. Stop the film at any point in order to emphasize a key point or main idea.

Discussion: Turn off the projection equipment. Do not rewind the film until the class has ended, if possible, in order to maintain attention of the group. Provide for proper light and ventilation for any follow up desk work. Rearrange the seating if necessary. Allow for any questions which might have been stimulated by the film. Insure that the main concepts presented in the motion picture were clearly understood by all students. Make proper application of the information to previous, present, and future class work. Note general impressions of the film for later use.

Advantages and Values

The film:

Enriches learning by presenting a series or sequence of meaningful experience involving motion.

Can enlarge or reduce the actual size of objects and present processes that might not otherwise be possible to duplicate.

Is innately attention-getting, generally heightens interest and motivation, and offers a satisfying aesthetic experience based upon dramatization and emotional appeal.

Can transcend the barriers of time, complexity, and space and bring the past, present, and probable future into the classroom.

Heightens reality by individualizing experiences of the outside world and promotes a greater understanding of abstract relationships and concepts.

Limitations and Problems

Films may be too general in nature, too lengthy and time consuming, or too complex for the specific situation.

The effective use of the film requires special skill and knowledge in the use of projection equipment.

Films may present incorrect time or size concepts and result in distorted impressions and conclusions without additional clarification.

The scheduling of appropriate films and equipment is often difficult and time-consuming.

A film too frequently is used as a substitute rather than a supplement for other more practical direct experiences.

Examples

Through the use of motion pictures it is possible to see reconstructions of famous historical events, life in other lands, and various abstract relationships. Films create a common denominator of experience through which reality can be achieved, processes explained, and situations reproduced. Many excellent films are listed in a number of film guides and catalogs. Some teachers or school districts have developed home-made pictures for instructional purposes.

Some of the problems associated with efficient film use already have been identified. Other considerations are indicated in the following example:

> . . . They should know what it is about, how it fits into the material being studied, and what they may expect to get out of it. As a film is being shown, it is often helpful for them to take notes, jotting down questions that come to mind or points to discuss. In order to prepare a group to get the most out of a film, you, the teacher, should preferably have seen it, made notes on it, and planned how best to use it.

> At times you may want to ask a class to take the responsibility of helping to evaluate films for use with future classes. This procedure gives students a realization that their judgment is respected and valued; it also makes them watch films more carefully, critically, and objectively. Thus, after a film has been shown and discussed, you might ask how many of the group would recommend that it be used again next year . . .[5]

Slides

Several types of slides are used for instructional purposes. Lantern slides are the pioneer of projected visual materials. They consist of three and one half by four inch standard slides made of clear or etched glass or plastic. Drawings, printing, typing, and other illustrative material is placed on the slide which is then projected on a screen for viewing purposes. Two by two inch slides of a photographic nature have largely replaced the lantern slide in many schools. Each type of slide, however, has certain advantages for projection purposes. The use of slides is limited only by the imagination and initiative of the teacher.

---

[5] *Guidebook for Teen-Agers,* copyright © 1955 by Scott, Foresman and Co., p. 33.

Procedural Steps

Selection of subject matter: The content to be developed should be pertinent to the lesson and contribute to further understanding. It should meet established objectives and lend itself to slide projection.

Arrangement: Slides may be purchased or hand-constructed from clear or etched glass, plastic, cellophane, and other transparent materials. Pens, inks, colors, and other materials should be obtained. Collect illustrative materials that might easily be copied or produced into slides. Photographic slide production requires proper lightₐ ₐg, exposure time, and photographic equipment.

Construction: Sets of lantern or photographic slides on specific topics may be purchased ready-made from numerous sources. For home-made lantern slides, an appropriate object may be traced directly on the slide with pencil and then colored with India ink, crayon, acetate ink, colored pencil, special slide ink, water colors, or other materials. When the slide is completed, the design should be covered with clear glass and bound at the edges with one half inch gummed tape. A thumb mark placed in the lower left hand corner of the slide can serve as a guide for later projection. Photographic slides can be easily produced by using a 35 mm camera under proper conditions.

Preview: Rehearse the lesson and the use of slide materials. Look for any errors, omissions, or inconsistencies on the slides as they are projected. Outline relevant comments, questions, and ideas for each slide to be used. Attempt to anticipate any problems or difficulties which are likely to arise.

Presentation: Set up the projector and screen and arrange the slides in the order of presentation before class begins. The lantern slide projector is used for lantern slides and the 35 mm slide projector for two by two slides. Briefly describe the purpose of the lesson, what to look for, and points to be emphasized. Allow time for questions, comments, and discussion during each slide showing where appropriate. Re-show any slides which might demand extra attention.

Evaluation: Summarize the material presented. Encourage student participation involving major idea formulation and the identification of key concepts illustrated in the lesson. Note ways to improve the overall presentation. Re-develop any slides that appeared to be weak or poorly constructed.

Advantages and Values

The slide:

Is relatively inexpensive to purchase, can be quite easily constructed and stored, and may be used countless times without deterioration.

Possesses an attention-focusing power which increases class interest and motivation.

Can be projected in a partially darkened room thus facilitating further class discussion and note taking.

May be enlarged to any desired size, repeatedly shown, and held on the screen for any period of time.

Is quite flexible in that a variety of printed, typed, or drawn materials can be presented in many different colors or combinations.

Limitations and Problems

Lantern slide projectors are somewhat bulky and difficult to manipulate easily.

Both the lantern and 35 mm projectors are costly to purchase.

The slide does not show motion and is somewhat limited as to the amount of complex material which can be presented.

Good slides require some artistic ability, imagination, time, photographic knowledge, and mechanical creativeness.

The slide generally necessitates additional narration and comment in order to be effective.

Examples

Careful planning is necessary to make the most efficient use of slides. The following example would indicate the effective application of the technique in a specific lesson:

In a demonstration lesson with a fourth-grade class, a teacher used a dozen slides to introduce the lesson. Four or five slides were used to show peoples and products during the development of the lesson, and another half dozen were used in summarizing. The lesson closed with a ten-minute quiz, for which the questions were written on slides and projected. In this lesson, the slides were worked into the lesson plan and used much the same as globes, maps, and sample products.[6]

Other Equipment Centered Procedures

Filmstrip. The filmstrip is a related sequence of transparent still pictures or images on a 35 mm film which are projected in progression on a screen. Filmstrips may be produced in black and white or color and are sometimes accompanied by recordings which carry narration, music, and sound effects. The filmstrip typically consists of from 20 to 50 frames or pictures each of which may or may not contain captions or titles.

Loop Film. The loop film is a short length of film spliced into a circle or loop. For viewing, the film is threaded into a projector to be shown continuously without rewinding. Special loop film projectors also are available. This process of repetition is especially valuable in emphasizing key points, illustrating basic skills, or in demonstrating ideas that are difficult to grasp.

Opaque Projector. The opaque projector is a device which utilizes reflected light to project non-transparent materials on a screen. It consists of a large metal box, illuminating lights, a blower to prevent the accumulation of excessive heat, a focusing lens, and mirrors which are arranged in such a manner as to reflect and magnify an image of the materials being shown. The modern opaque projector may possess a built-in pointer and a rotating platform which facilitates the viewing of materials that have been arranged in a fixed sequence. Any type of flat material may be used with the projector, including materials found in books and magazines.

Overhead Projector. An overhead projector is a device that reproduces an image on a screen by way of light reflection from a mirror through transparent plastic material. It has multiple uses for illustration purposes and lends itself well to utilization for many subject fields. An important advantage of the overhead projector

---

[6] Kinder, *op. cit.,* p. 104.

is that it can be operated by the instructor from the front of the room.

Radio. The radio is a well known device used to receive signals or sound by means of electric waves without a directly connecting wire. Both public and private broadcasts are available in many schools. Commercial or school sponsored programs with educational motives may be assigned for classroom or out-of-school listening. The production and utilization of programs developed by the class also might be feasible.

Recordings. The recording is a device used to record or duplicate sound. It may consist of a disk, cylinder, tape, or wire upon which sound has been recorded. The sound is then reproduced by playing the recording on a suitable machine designed for that purpose. The phonograph record, tape recording, transcription, and recording disk are common examples. Recordings help to enrich and broaden learning, form a bond between school life and the outside world, and increase student listening skills.

Tachistoscope. A special flashmeter or shutter-like attachment to the overhead projector provides a variation called the tachistoscope. It is used for controlled recognition exposures of a brief time—figures, words, sentences, and paragraphs. It is most frequently used in the teaching of spelling, reading, and arithmetic.

Teaching Machine. A teaching machine is a device which utilizes programmed materials for instructional purposes. It involves a fusion of learning and testing through a series of specially designed questions and answers presented in printed sequence on frames. Programmed textbooks and other programmed printed materials also are available in various subjects. The technique serves to organize subject matter into small and simple to more difficult steps and arranges them in a logical and cumulative progression.

Television. A television set is a device used to receive the reproduction of a scene or a picture. This is accomplished by means of converting light rays into electromagnetic waves and reconverting the waves into visible light rays. Educational television, through normal or closed circuit procedures, is receiving increasing attention as an instructional method. Video-tape recordings make it possible to preserve "master" shows for subsequent viewing and listening, in addition to student or teacher presentations. Teacher and class preparation and proper follow up is an essential and integral part of the success of educational television.

Glossary*

Anecdotal record: descriptive account of events, episodes, or circumstances in the daily life of the student.

Brainstorming: group technique designed to obtain a quantity of ideas on a subject.

Buzz session: designed to facilitate dividing a large class into smaller groups for discussion purposes.

Cartoon: interpretive drawing that usually exaggerates or satirizes to emphasize a point.

Case study: detailed account of situations or individual problems as a basis for instruction.

Check list: device used to help determine the existence or status of certain conditions or circumstances.

Closed circuit television: modified form of television in which signals are transmitted by coaxial cables rather than sound waves.

Cluster group: another name for the buzz session.

Colloquium: discussion involving two panel groups, one composed of authoritative resource persons and the other of selected class members.

Counseling: individualized and personalized assistance, advice, or deliberation designed to promote better student adjustment and achievement.

---

* Adapted from various references, especially Carter V. Good (ed.), *Dictionary of Education*, 2nd ed. New York: McGraw-Hill Book Company, 1959, 676 pp.

Creative writing: spontaneous and imaginative composition in the form of stories, verse, or other means of self-expression.

Cutaway: term applied to a model that has a part of the exterior removed to facilitate a view and study of the interior.

Debate: clearly defined pro and con discussion of an issue or question.

Demonstration: visual and verbal explanation of an idea, process, fact, or phenomenon.

Diagram: type of drawing that utilizes lines and conventional geometrical symbols.

Diorama: small three-dimensional representation incorporating symbolic or real specimens or materials.

Drama: term meaning to do or act, and involving an active form of expression.

Etched glass: a type of glass used for making lantern slides which has one side etched or treated in a special manner.

Excursion: another name for the field trip.

Exhibit: display of materials ordinarily of a three-dimensional nature.

Felt board: another name for the flannel board.

Flannel board: board covered with any of several types of fabric, including felt or flannel to which pictures, objects, or other materials may be adhered.

Flip chart: set of charts arranged in a series and viewed in a predetermined sequence.

Forum: two or more presentations to a group on the same subject or topic with audience participation.

Graph: presentation of interrelated statistical information by means of lines, dots, pictures, or other symbols.

Graphics: art and science of utilizing charts, displays, diagrams, maps, posters, and other printed or diagrammatic symbols.

Group dynamics: method of social research designed to provide a comprehensive and systematic understanding of group phenomena.

Guidance: assistance designed to facilitate an assessment of individual abilities, capabilities, and limitations.

Indoctrination: presentation of predetermined opinions or proved ideas without great concern for reasoning.

Instruction: practice of providing direction in the learning process, emphasizing the imparting of information, knowledge, or skill. Sometimes used in a more limited sense than the term "teaching."

Instructional materials: materials used in schools for instructional purposes.

Inventory: instrument used to ascertain the status of an aspect of student behavior, community activity, or the instructional program.

Laboratory experimentation: series of tests undertaken to discover an underlying principle or to prove or disprove a point.

Lantern slide: 3½ x 4 inch glass or plastic slide used for projection purposes.

Learning: a consistent change in behavior as the result of experience.

Loop film: short length of film spliced into a circle or loop and threaded into a projector for continuous viewing.

Magnetic board: board of sheet metal to which small magnets will adhere for instructional purposes.

Marionette: a string-manipulated puppet.

Method: process which involves a rational ordering or balancing of the elements which enter into the educative function—purposes, nature of the learner, materials of instruction, and the total learning situation. "Teaching method" generally is considered synonymous with "instructional method."

Methodology: science and theory concerned with the description, place, kinds, and appraisal of methods or principles of procedure used in teaching.

Mobile: series of delicately balanced and suspended objects.

Mock-up: simulated or contrived three-dimensional model.

Mural: photographic or graphic decoration placed on a wall.

Opaque projector: device designed to project non-transparent flat materials.

Overhead projector: instrument that projects an image on a screen by means of light reflection through a transparency from a mirror.

Pageant: drama usually based on local history and ordinarily performed outdoors.

Pamphlet: paperbound document of limited length.

Pantomime: type of dramatization emphasizing gestures and actions without verbal communication.

Play: carefully rehearsed dramatic presentation using a script, costumes, and an elaborate setting.

Playlet: shortened and less elaborate version of a play.

Problem solving: analyzation of a problem culminating in a scientifically determined conclusion or solution.

Procedure: deliberate and relatively concise approach, manner, or course of action used in instruction. Ordinarily construed to be more specific than teaching "method," but broader than teaching "technique."

Programmed learning: organized subject matter arranged for sequential and progressive learning. Usually used in connection with a teaching machine.

Project: planned individual or class undertaking designed to compile information, collect objects, construct materials, or create something.

Projection: use of a stimulus to encourage spontaneous and uninhibited discussion or reaction to a problem or situation. Also applies to the process of "projecting" material on a screen for viewing.

Psychodrama: unrehearsed and spontaneous acting out of a personally perplexing problem or situation by the individual.

Questionnaire: type of survey form used to obtain specific information from responses to selected questions.

Rating scale: device used to record judgments of observations.

Resource person: another name for the outside speaker.

Role playing: spontaneous, unrehearsed, and on-the-spot acting out of a situation or problem.

Self-test: series of questions or exercises designed to measure personal knowledge, skill, or other aspects of behavior.

Skit: brief satirical, comic, or humorous dramatic presentation.

Slide: 2 x 2 inch slide of a photographic type; also see lantern slide.

Sociodrama: unrehearsed and spontaneous dramatization dealing with some socially significant problem or issue.

Sociogram: chart-type device used to help indicate relationships between individuals in a group.

Survey: scientific analysis of existing practices, programs, or processes.

Symbolism: representation of ideas, objects, or meanings by signs, labels, or words.

Symposium: presentation consisting of two or more brief discourses dealing with different aspects of the same general topic or subject.

Tableau: still-life representation of persons against a background.

Tachistoscope: overhead projector with a flashmeter or shutter-like attachment for controlled recognition exposures of a brief time.

Tackboard: another name for the bulletin board.

Teaching: art and science of instructing. Act of providing activities, materials, direction, and guidance to facilitate learning, in either formal or informal situations.

Teaching machine: device that utilizes programmed materials of a sequential nature that are presented in "frames."

Technique: details or specific elements of procedure required in the execution of instruction or manner of performance. Essential basic skills in an art, activity, or production.

Transparency: clear or frosted plastic material used to facilitate the projection of images on a screen.

Video tape: sound and picture recording of a television show used for rebroadcast at a later time.

Workshop: group gathering in which individuals study problems that are of mutual interest or concern.

Bibliography

Chapter I

Association for Supervision and Curriculum Development, *Human Variability and Learning,* 1961 Yearbook. Washington, D. C.: National Education Association, 1961.

Breckenridge, M. E. and M. N. Murphy, *Growth and Development of the Young Child,* 7th ed. Philadelphia: W. B. Saunders Co., 1963.

Bruner, Jerome S., *The Process of Education.* Cambridge, Mass.: Harvard University Press, 1961.

Burton, William H. and Helen Heffernan, *The Step Beyond: Creativity.* Washington, D. C.: Elementary-Kindergarten-Nursery Education, National Education Association, 1964.

Crescimbeni, Joseph and Raymond J. Mammarelli, "Hidden Hazards in Teaching," *NEA J.,* 54:31, January, 1965.

Cyphert, F. R., "Freedom of Method: Boon or Bane of Teaching," *High School J.,* Vol. 45, October, 1961.

Field, Jane T., "What the Books Don't Tell you," *NEA J.,* 53:58-59, October, 1964.

Filbin, Robert L. and Stefan Vogel, *So You're Going to be a Teacher.* Great Neck, N.Y.: Barron's Educational Series Inc., 1962.

Gage, N. L. (ed.), *Handbook of Research on Teaching.* Chicago: Rand McNally & Co., 1963.

Hanna, Lavone, Gladys Potter, and Neva Hagaman, *Unit Teaching in the Elementary School.* New York: Holt, Rinehart and Winston, Inc., 1963.

Harris, Theodore L. and Wilson E. Schwahn, *Selected Readings on the Learning Process.* New York: Oxford University Press, Inc., 1961.

Havighurst, Robert J., *Developmental Tasks and Education.* New York: David McKay Co., Inc., 1962.

Hughes, Marie M., "What Teachers Do and the Way They Do It," *NEA J.*, 53:11-13, September, 1964.

Jacobs, Leland B., *The Image of the Teacher.* Washington, D. C.: National Education Association, 1964.

Lewis, Gertrude M. *The Evaluation of Teaching.* Washington, D. C.: Department of Elementary-Kindergarten-Nursery Education, National Education Association, 1966.

Miller, William C. and Albert L. Goldberg, "Getting the Most from the Newer Media," *NEA J.*, 53:30-31, April, 1964.

Passow, A. Harry and Robert R. Leeper (eds.), *Intellectual Development: Another Look.* Washington, D. C.: Association for Supervision and Curriculum Development, National Education Association, 1964.

Planning and Organizing for Teaching, NEA Project on Instruction, Washington, D. C.: National Education Association, 1963.

Raths, Louis E., Merrill Harmin, and Sidney B. Simon, *Values and Teaching.* Columbus, Ohio: Charles E. Merrill Publishing Company, 1966.

Ray, Henry W., "Freeing Pupils from the Sit-Look-Listen Syndrome," *NEA J.*, 56:8-10, April, 1967.

Stuart, Marion F., *Neurophysiological Insights into Teaching.* Palo Alto, Calif.: Pacific Books, Publishers, 1963.

Thomas, R. Murray, *Judging Student Progress,* rev. ed. New York: David McKay Co., Inc., 1962.

Torkelson, Gerald M. and Emily A. Torkelson, "How Mechanized Should the Classroom Be?" *NEA J.*, 56:28-30, March, 1967.

Trump, J. Lloyd, *New Directions to Quality Education,* Commission on the Experimental Study of the Utilization of the Staff in the Secondary School. Washington, D. C.: National Association of Secondary-School Principals, 1960.

Wenzel, Evelyn, "What Is a Creative Teacher?" *NEA J.*, 53:8-10, September, 1964.

Woodruff, Asahel D., *Basic Concepts of Teaching.* San Francisco: Chandler Publishing Co., 1961.

Chapter 2

Brainstorming

"Brainstorming—A Creative Problem Solving Technique," *J. Communication,* 7:29-32, Autumn, 1957.

McCloskey, William R., "Brainstorming," *Home Economics, 49:*705-06, November, 1957.

Osborne, Alexander, *Applied Imagination,* 3rd ed. New York: Charles Scribner's Sons, 1957.

Buzz Session

Bradford, Leland P., "Developing Potentialities Through Class Groups," *Teachers College Record, 61:*443-50, May, 1960.

Jenkins, Gladys G., William W. Bauer, and Helen S. Shacter, *Techniques for Group Guidance with Teen-Agers.* Chicago: Scott, Foresman & Company, 1957.

Strong, Ruth, *Group Work in Education.* New York: Harper & Row, Publishers, 1958.

Case Study

McNair, M. P. (ed.), *The Case Method at the Harvard Business School.* New York: McGraw-Hill Book Company, 1954.

Oliver, Donald and Susan Baker, "The Case Method," *Social Education,* 23:25-29, January, 1959.

Pigors, Paul and Faith Pigors, *Case Method in Human Relations: The Incident Process.* New York: McGraw-Hill Book Company, 1961.

Committee Work

Clark, Betty Jean, "Committee Assignments Can Be Challenging and Fun," *Adult Leadership, 10:*289-313, April, 1962.

Koess, W. A., "Reliability, Sex Differences, and Validity in the Leaderless Group Discussion Technique," *Applied Psychology,* Vol. 45, October, 1961.

Shaw, Archibald B., "Committees—Bane or Blessing?", *Overview,* 1:11-13, October, 1960.

Discussion

Barnlund, Dean C. and Franklyn S. Haiman, *The Dynamics of Discussion.* Boston: Houghton Mifflin Company, 1960.

Fausti, R. P., and A. H. Luker, "Phenomenological Approach to Discussion," *Speech Teacher, 14*:19-23, January, 1965.

Harnack, R. Victor and Thorrel B. Fest, *Group Discussion: Theory and Technique.* New York: Appleton-Century-Crofts, 1964.

Litchen, Ruth E., *How to Use Group Discussion,* rev. ed. How to Do It Series, No. 6. Washington, D. C.: National Council for the Social Studies, 1965.

Ohles, J. F., "Mechanics of Discussion," *Secondary Education, 40*:16-18, January, 1965.

Watkins, Lloyd I., "Some Problems and Solutions in Teaching Group Discussion," *Speech Teacher, 10*:211-14, September, 1961.

Xavier, Mary, "Discussion: A Useful Teaching Method," *Clearing House, 38*:33-37, September, 1963.

Problem Solving

Briggs, Frances, "The Problem-Centered Approaches to Teaching," *High School J., 46*:196-204, March, 1963.

Elmore, C. W., Orson Keeslar, and C. E. Parrish, "Why Not Try the Problem Solving Approach?" *Science Teacher,* Vol. 28, December, 1961.

Mills, Lester C. and Peter M. Dean, *Problem-Solving Methods in Science Teaching.* New York: Bureau of Publications, Teachers College, Columbia University, 1960.

Muessig, Raymond H. and Vincent R. Rogers, "Building Problem-

Solving Attitudes and Skills in the Primary Grades," *NEA J.*, 50: 38-40, October, 1961.

Smith, William S., *Group Problem-Solving Through Discussion*, rev. ed. Indianapolis: The Bobbs-Merrill Co., Inc., 1965.

Other Group Procedures

Cartwright, Dorwin and Alvin Zander (eds.), *Group Dynamics: Research and Theory*, 2nd. ed. Evanston, Ill.: Harper & Row, Publishers, 1960.

Conducting Workshops and Institutes, Leadership Pamphlet No. 9. Chicago: Adult Education Association, 1956.

DeLong, Arthur R., "Values and Dangers of the Sociogram," *Understanding the Child*, 36:24-28, January, 1957.

Gulley, Halbert E., *Discussion, Conference and Group Process.* New York: Holt, Rinehart and Winston, Inc., 1960.

Hoover, K. H., "Panel Discussions Can Be Effective," *Clearing House*, 36:14-15, September, 1961.

Hullfish, H. Gordon and Philip G. Smith, *Reflective Thinking: The Method of Education.* New York: Dodd, Mead & Co., 1961.

Keith, Davis, *Human Relations at Work.* New York: McGraw-Hill Book Company, 1962.

Northway, Mary L. and Lindsay Weld, *Sociometric Testing.* Toronto: University of Toronto Press, 1957.

Purvell, E. J., "Group Dynamics in Social Studies," *The Instructor*, 72:94-97, October, 1962.

Ross, J. A., "Group Discussion in High School Needed," *Ohio Schools*, 39:19-22, November, 1961.

Savage, John F., "Elaborate Thinking—Done Better in Groups," *Elementary School J.*, 64:434-37, May, 1964.

Thelen, Herbert A. and Dorothy Stock (eds.), *Understanding How Groups Work,* Leadership Pamphlet No. 4. Chicago: Adult Education Association, 1956.

Watkins, L. I., "Some Problems and Solutions in Teaching Group Discussion," *Speech Teacher*, Vol. 10, September, 1961.

Wood, Donald I., *A Call to Order.* Washington: National Association of Secondary-School Principals, 1964.

Chapter 3

Game

Coleman, James S., "Learning Through Games," *NEA J., 56*:69-70, January, 1967.

How We Do It Gamebook, 3rd ed. Washington, D. C.: American Association for Health, Physical Education and Recreation, 1964.

Kraus, Richard, *The Family Book of Games*. New York: McGraw-Hill Book Company, 1960.

Role Playing

Boyd, Gertrude, "Role Playing," *Social Education, 21*:267-69, October, 1957.

Frank, Helen, "Role Playing and Tape Recording Add New Dimensions to Class Discussions," *Marriage and Family Living, 22*:181-82, May, 1960.

Greenberg, Morton, "Role Playing to Motivate Acceptable Behavior," *Health Education J., 24*:6-7, March, 1961.

Klein, Alan F., *How to Use Role Playing Effectively*. New York: Association Press, 1959.

Skit

Fischer, Beatrice T. and Irene B. Harms, "Developing a Health Play in the Classroom," *Health Education J., 22*:6-7, November, 1959.

Liebowitz, Sandra, "Skits, Games, and a Magic Carpet," *NEA J., 50*:25-27, December, 1961.

Siks, Geraldine B., *Creative Dramatics*. New York: Harper & Row, Publishers, 1958.

Wittich, Walter A. and Gertie H. Halstad, *Educators Guide to Free Tapes, Scripts, and Transcriptions,* rev. each August. Randolph, Wis.: Educators Progress Service, 1965.

Sociodrama

Graham, Grace, "Sociodrama as a Teaching Technique," *Education Digest,* 26:44-46, March, 1961.

Gronlund, Norman E., *Sociometry in the Classroom.* New York: Harper & Row, Publishers, 1959.

Jennings, Helen H., *Sociometry in Group Relations,* rev. ed. Washington, D. C.: American Council on Education, 1959.

Zeleny, Leslie D., *How to Use the Sociodrama,* rev. ed., How to Do It Series, No. 20. Washington, D. C.: National Council for the Social Studies, 1964.

Storytelling

Nichols, Ralph G. and Leonard Stevens, *Are You Listening?.* New York: McGraw-Hill Book Company, 1958.

Petluck, Robert F. and Lillian Glassburg, "From Fantasy to Learning," *Audio-Visual Instruction,* 2:274-75, December, 1957.

Tooze, Ruth, *Storytelling.* Englewood Cliffs, N.J.: Prentice-Hall, Inc., 1959.

Other Dramatic Procedures

Ashton, Dudley, *Rhythmic Activities, Grades K-6.* Washington, D. C.: American Association for Health, Physical Education and Recreation, 1964.

Batchelder, Marjorie and Virginia L. Comer, *Puppets and Plays.* New York: Harper & Row, Publishers, 1956.

Chase, Mary, "The Magic of Poetry," *NEA J.,* 53:8-11, December, 1964.

Cutler, Bruce and Richard J. Meyer, "Presenting Poetry on Television," *National Association of Educational Broadcasters J., 23:* 40, September-October, 1964.

Fitzgerald, R. Bernard, "Creative Music Teaching in the Elementary School," *NEA J.*, 53:42-43, December, 1964.

Krone, Beatrice, *Music Participation in the Elementary School*. Englewood Cliffs, N.J.: Prentice-Hall, Inc., 1957.

Schwartz, John C., "Introduce Paper Marionettes to Your Class," *The Instructor, 64*:35-36, January, 1955.

Walter, Nona W., *Let Them Write Poetry*. New York: Holt, Rinehart and Winston, Inc., 1962.

Chapter 4

Creative Writing

Ellsworth, Ruth, "Critical Thinking," *National Elementary Principal,* 42:24-29, May, 1963.

Getzels, Jacob W. and Philip W. Jackson, *Creativity and Intelligence.* New York: John Wiley & Sons, Inc., 1962.

Payne, Lucile V., "Teaching Students to Write," *NEA J., 55*:28-30, November, 1966.

Laboratory Experimentation

Hutchinson, John S. and Donald W. Stotler, *Frontiers for Change: Using the Laboratory Method.* Washington, D. C.: National Education Association, 1963.

Palmer, William F., "The Laboratory Approach to Teaching," *High School J., 46*:204-17, March, 1963.

Vrana, R. S., "Laboratory Work, Grades Seven and Eight," *Science Teacher,* Vol. 28, November, 1961.

Oral Report

Adams, Harlen M. and Thomas C. Pollock, *Speak Up*. New York: The Macmillan Company, 1956.

Hoover, Kenneth H., "Improving Oral Reports," *Clearing House, 33*: 357-58, February, 1959.

Johnson, Lois V., "The Process of Oral Reporting," *Elementary English,* 35:309-13, May, 1958.

Survey

Moser, Claus A., *Survey Methods in Social Investigation.* London: William Heinemann Ltd., 1958.

Parten, Mildred B., *Surveys, Polls, and Samples.* New York: Harper & Row, Publishers, 1950.

Warren, Roland L., *Studying Your Community.* New York: Russell Sage Foundation, 1955.

Other Student Oriented Procedures

Butman, Alexander, Donald Reis, and David Sohn (eds.), *Paperbacks in the Schools.* New York: Bantam Books, Inc., 1963.

Carlton, Lessie and Robert H. Moore, "Individualized Reading," *NEA J., 53*:11-12, November, 1964.

Cartwright, William H., *How to Use a Textbook,* rev. ed., How to Do It Series, No. 2. Washington, D. C.: National Council for the Social Studies, 1964.

Condit, Louise, "Your School Can Have a Museum," *The Instructor,* 65:15-16, January, 1956.

Cummings, Howard H. and Harry Bard, *How to Use Daily Newspapers,* rev. ed., How to Do It Series, No. 5. Washington, D. C.: National Council for the Social Studies, 1965.

Davis, Jerry B., "Are the Doers Learning?" *Clearing House, 37*:489, April, 1963.

Dawson, G. G., "Experiment in Teacher-Pupil Planning," *Social Education, 24*:325-28, November, 1960.

Deason, Hilary J., *A Guide to Science Reading.* New York: The New American Library, Inc., 1963.

Elementary Reading List Committee, *Adventuring with Books: A Reading List for Elementary Grades.* Washington, D. C.: National Council of Teachers of English, 1960.

Graham, M. D., "Your Librarian Will Collect Curriculum Materials," *The Instructor,* Vol. 71, November, 1961.

How to Locate Useful Government Publications, rev. ed., How to Do It Series, No. 9. Washington, D. C.: National Council for the Social Studies, 1964.

Hullfish, H. Gordon and Philip G. Smith, *Reflective Thinking: The Method of Education.* New York: Dodd, Mead & Co., 1961.

Kersh, B. Y., "Motivating Effect of Learning by Directed Discovery," *J. Educational Psychology,* Vol. 53, April, 1962.

Klein, Anna L., "Let's Lower Sights," *NEA J.,* 53:17-18, November, 1964.

Milgaard, K. G., "Science for Human Beings," *Educational Leadership,* Vol. 20, January, 1963.

Moscow, David H., "Individualized Instruction with Paperbacks," *NEA J.,* 53:21-22, April, 1964.

Chapter 5

Current Events

Cummings, Howard H. and Harry Bard, *How to Use Daily Newspapers,* rev. ed., How to Do It Series, No. 5. Washington, D. C.: National Council for the Social Studies, 1965.

"Getting the Most from Newspapers," *NEA J.,* 50:32-33, December, 1961.

Miller, Edith F., "Stimulate Reading with Current Events," *Grade Teacher,* 79:19-22, October, 1961.

Demonstration

Berger, Edward J., "How to Give a Demonstration," *Industrial Arts and Vocational Education,* 31:35-36, September, 1960.

Ruke, D. S., "Medical Demonstration Will Offer Rare Opportunities," *Audiovisual Instruction,* Vol. 7, February, 1962.

Smith, Hayden R., "Show and Tell How It Works," *The Clearing House,* 36:422-24, March, 1962.

Swales, Willis, Jr., "Demonstrate and Teach," *School Science and Mathematics,* 61:98-100, February, 1961.

Field Trip

How to Conduct a Field Trip, rev. ed., How to Do It Series, No. 10. Washington, D. C.: National Council for the Social Studies, 1965.

Koch, Dorothy C., "Class Trip," *NEA J.,* 53:17-20, April, 1964.

Ruth, F. S., "Field Trips: Why and How," *American Biology Teacher,* Vol. 24, January, 1962.

Sommers, N. L., "Nature Hikes for More than Fun," *School Activities,* Vol. 34, November, 1962.

Lecture

Carr, R. W., "Lecture Method in the Junior High School," *Social Studies,* Vol. 53, January, 1962.

Pulliam, Lloyd, "The Lecture—Are We Reviving Discredited Teaching Methods?" *Phi Delta Kappan,* 44:382-84, May, 1963.

Taylor, H. O., "Comparison of the Effectiveness of a Lecture Method and a Small-Group Discussion Method of Teaching High School Biology," *Science Education,* Vol. 43, December, 1959.

Outside Speaker

Gross, Richard, *How to Handle Controversial Issues,* rev. ed., How to Do It Series, No. 12. Washington, D. C.: National Council for the Social Studies, 1964.

Haakenson, Robert, *How to Handle the Q and A.* Philadelphia: Smith, Kline and French Laboratories, 1962.

How to Utilize Community Resources, rev. ed., How to Do It Series, No. 11. Washington, D. C.: National Council for the Social Studies, 1964.

Smith, P. G., "Art of Asking Questions," *Reading Teacher,* Vol. 15, September, 1961.

Other Teacher Initiated Procedures

Arbuckle, Dugald S., *Counseling: An Introduction.* Boston: Allyn & Bacon, Inc., 1961.

Bingham, Walter V. and Bruce V. Moore, *How to Interview,* 4th ed., rev. New York: Harper & Row, Publishers, 1959.

Breslow, Alice P., "Adolescent Guidance," *J. School Health,* 22:178-86, May, 1962.

Bresvinick, S. L., "Effective Daily Lesson Plans," *Clearing House,* Vol. 34, March, 1960.

Chauncey, Henry, "How Objective Are Objective Tests?" *School Management,* 6:133, March, 1962.

Cohen, Benjamin, "Guidance and Counseling in Groups," *NEA J.,* 55: 38-39, October, 1966.

Conferences That Work, Leadership Pamphlet No. 11. Chicago: Adult Education Association, 1956.

Elliot, R. W., "Team Teaching: Effective In-Service Training," *Am. School Board J.,* Vol. 144, February, 1962.

Freer, James J., "The Teacher as Counselor," *Education,* 82:336, February, 1962.

Haakenson, Robert, *You Are the Next Speaker.* Philadelphia: Smith, Kline and French Laboratories, 1962.

Hoppock, Anne, "Team Teaching: Form Without Substance?" *NEA J.,* 50:47-48, April, 1961.

Jones, Arthur J., *Principles of Guidance,* 5th ed. New York: McGraw-Hill Book Company, 1963.

Leuchtenburg, Dennis, "Testing is a Big Part of Teaching," *NEA J.,* 53:55-56, October, 1964.

Loughary, John W., *Counseling in Secondary Schools.* New York: Harper & Row, Publishers, 1961.

Mass, B. S., "How to Teach a Unit," *The Instructor,* Vol. 70, September, 1960.

Sanders, Norris M., *Classroom Questions: What Kinds?* New York: Harper & Row, Publishers, 1966.

Shalowitz, Elaine L., "Our School is Trying Team Teaching," *NEA J.,* 53:45-46, May, 1964.

Thomas, R. M., *Judging Student Progress*, 2nd. ed. New York: David McKay Co., Inc., 1960.

Tips for Planning Meetings. New York: National Pharmaceutical Council, Inc., 1963.

Van Til, William, "How *Not* to Make an Assignment," *NEA J.,* 53:49-51, October, 1964.

Wiebe, A. J., "High School Guidance in 1970," *J. Secondary Education,* Vol. 37, January, 1962.

Wood, Dorothy A., *Test Construction*. Columbus, Ohio: Charles E. Merrill Publishing Company, 1960.

Chapter 6

Bulletin Board

Burgert, R. H., "Bulletin Boards: Planning," *The Instructor,* 72:64, October, 1962.

Fox, W. E., "Care and Feeding of Bulletin Boards," *Education, 83:* 363-65, February, 1963.

McMahan, Marie and Stella Dickerman, "Bulletin Boards for End of School," *The Instructor,* 71:77, June, 1962.

Randall, Reino and Edward C. Haines, *Bulletin Boards and Displays*. Worcester, Mass.: Davis Publications, Inc., 1961.

Chart

Charts. San Bernardino, Calif.: Office of the Superintendent, San Bernardino County Schools, 1957.

Kinder, James S., "The Use of Graphic Materials in Teaching," *Education,* 77:299-302, January, 1957.

Meeks, Martha F., *Lettering Techniques*. Austin: Visual Instruction Bureau, University of Texas, 1960.

Exhibit

Duffy, Joseph W., "Dioramas," *The Instructor, 66*: 29-30, January, 1957.

Museum Technique in Fundamental Education, Educational Studies, Document No. 17. New York: UNESCO Publications Department, 1957.

Olson, Robert H., "Make a Three-Way Display for Learning," *Teaching Tools, 3*: 132-33, Summer, 1956.

White, James B., "Bulletin Board Exhibits," *Education, 84*:373-76, February, 1964.

Flannel Board

Barnard, D. P., "How to Use a Flannel Board," *Industrial Arts and Vocational Education, 50*: 26-27, November, 1961.

"Fun with Flannel Boards," *Grade Teacher, 83*: 92-94, April, 1966.

Jenkins, P. R., "Flannelboards, Friend or Foe," *J. Religious Education, 38*:23-25, February, 1962.

"Making a Flannel Board," *The Instructor, 76*:32, October, 1966.

Other Material Focused Procedures

Association for Supervision and Curriculum Development, *Curriculum Materials.* Washington, D. C.: National Education Association, 1961.

Brown, James W., Richard B. Lewis, and Fred C. Harcleroad, *A-V Instruction: Materials and Methods,* 2nd ed. New York: McGraw-Hill Book Company, 1964.

Coplan, Kate, *Poster Ideas and Bulletin Board Techniques: For Libraries and Schools.* New York: Oceana Publications, Inc., 1962.

Dever, Esther, *Sources of Free and Inexpensive Educational Materials,* rev. ed. Grafton, W. Va.: P. O. Box 186, 1963.

Division of Surveys and Field Services, *Free and Inexpensive Learning Materials.* Nashville, Tenn.: George Peabody College for Teachers, issued periodically.

Educators Guide to Free Science Materials, Educators Guide to Free Social Studies Materials, and *Elementary Teachers Guide to Free Curriculum Materials.* Randolph, Wis.: Educators Progress Service, issued periodically.

Espig, Florence, "3-D Figures on Posters," *The Instructor,* 70:43, November, 1960.

Freedman, Florence B. and Esther L. Berg, *Classroom Teachers' Guide to Audio-Visual Materials.* Philadelphia: Chilton Book Company, 1961.

Free Learning Materials for Classroom Use. Cedar Falls, Iowa: Extension Service, State College of Iowa, 1963.

Hanna, Nancy W. and John M. Geston, "How to Use Professional Periodicals," *NEA J.,* 56:63-64, February, 1967.

Horn, George F., *Posters: Designing, Making, Reproducing.* Worcester, Mass.: Davis Publications Inc., 1964.

How to Introduce Maps and Globes, rev. ed., How to Do It Series, No. 12. Washington, D. C.: National Council for the Social Studies, 1965.

Kingery, W. D., *Introduction to Ceramics.* New York: John Wiley & Sons, Inc., 1960.

Minor, Edward, *Simplified Techniques for Preparing Visual Materials.* New York: McGraw-Hill Book Company, 1962.

The Audio-Visual Index. Detroit: Audio-Visual Research Institute, 1961.

"The Flexible Displayboard," *Education,* 86:436-37, March, 1966.

Woolever, John D., "Using Cartoons in the Classroom," *School Science and Mathematics,* 50:255-58, April, 1950.

Chapter 7

Chalkboard

George, E. A., "It's a Blank Until You Use It," *Internatl. J. of Religious Educ.,* 38:10-11, 25, May, 1962.

Grassell, E. Milton, "Chalk and Chalkboards," *Teaching Tools*, 5: 72-73, Spring, 1958.

"Improving the Use of the Chalkboard," 35 mm filmstrip. Columbus, Ohio: The Ohio State University, 1956.

Film

Audio-Visual Center, *Catalog of Educational Motion Pictures*. Bloomington: Indiana University, yearly supplements, 1964.

Educational Film Guide. New York: H. W. Wilson Co., published quarterly.

Film Festival Guide. New York: Educational Film Library Association, 1964.

Horkheimer, Mary F. and John W. Diffor (eds.), *Educators Guide to Free Films*. Randolph, Wis.: Educators Progress Service, published periodically.

How to Use a Motion Picture, rev. ed., How to Do It Series, No. 1. Washington, D. C.: National Council for the Social Studies, 1965.

Reid, Surley, Anita Carpenter, and A. R. Daugherty, *A Directory of 3,660 16 mm Film Libraries,* U. S. Department of Health, Education, and Welfare, Bulletin No. 4. Washington, D. C.: Government Printing Office, 1964.

Opaque Projector

Blanc, Sam S., "Preparing Opaque Projection Materials," *Teaching Tools*, 3: 172-73, Fall, 1956.

Green, Ivah, "Blow It Up with the Opaque Projector," *Teaching Tools,* 5: 22-23, Winter, 1958.

White, F. A., "The Opaque Projector—A Real Aid," *Education,* 77: 290-92, January, 1957.

Slides

"Color Slides Used with TV," *National Association of Educational Broadcasters J.*, 23: 77, March-April, 1964.

Lehman, Frederick M., "Creative Techniques for Exciting Slides," *Audio-Visual Instruction,* 2:264-65, December, 1957.

Pillet, Roger, "French with Slides and Tapes—A Reappraisal," *Elementary School J.,* November, 1964.

Other Equipment Centered Procedures

Bannerman, R. LeRoy, "Creativity in Radio," *National Association of Educational Broadcasters J.,* 23:11, July-August, 1964.

Costello, Laurence F. and George N. Gordon, *Teaching with Television.* New York: Hastings House, Publishers, Inc., 1961.

Davis, Gladys D., "The Challenge of TV Teaching," *NEA J.,* 55:10-11, 70, April, 1966.

Duker, Sam, *Listening Bibliography.* New York: Scarecrow Press, Inc., 1964.

Eboch, Sidney C., *Operating Audio-Visual Materials.* San Francisco: Chandler Publishing Co., 1960.

Fry, Edward B., *Teaching Machines and Programmed Instruction.* New York: McGraw-Hill Book Company, 1963.

Horn, George F., *How to Prepare Visual Materials for School Use.* Worcester, Mass.: Davis Publications, Inc., 1963.

Klaw, Spencer, "What Can We Learn from the Teaching Machines?" *The Reporter,* 27:19-26, July 19, 1962.

Lange, Phil C., "Selection and Use of Programmed Learning Materials," *NEA J.,* 53:28-29, April, 1964.

Maier, Milton H. and Paul I. Jacobs, "Programed Learning—Some Recommendations and Results," *Bulletin of National Association of Secondary-School Principals,* 48:242-55, April, 1964.

Ofiesh, Gabriel D. and Wesley C. Meirhenry, *Trends in Programmed Instruction.* Washington, D. C.: Department of Audio-Visual Instruction, National Education Association, 1964.

Pearson, Mary D., *Recordings in the Public Library.* Chicago: American Library Association, 1963.

"Radio's Role in Instruction," *National Association of Educational Broadcasters J.,* 23:16, November-December, 1964.

Ramsey, Curtis P., "Curriculum Issues in Programmed Instruction," *Education*, 83:412-15, March, 1963.

Recordings for Children, New York Library Association. New York: Office of Children's Services, New York Public Library, 1964.

Rufsvold, Margaret and Carolyn Guss, *Guides to Newer Educational Media: Films, Filmstrips, Phono-Records, Radio, Slides, and Television.* Chicago: American Library Association, 1961.

Schramm, Wilbur, Jack Lyle, and Edwin B. Parker, *Television in the Lives of Our Children.* Stanford, Calif.: Stanford University Press, 1961.

Schultz, Morton J., *The Teacher and Overhead Projection.* Englewood Cliffs, N.J.: Prentice-Hall, Inc., 1965.

Selection and Use of Programmed Materials. Washington, D.C.: Department of Audio Visual Instruction, National Education Association, 1964.

Siggelkow, Richard A., *How to Use Recordings*, rev. ed., How to Do It Series, No. 8. Washington, D.C.: National Council for the Social Studies, 1964.

Silberman, Harry F., "Self-Teaching Devices and Programmed Materials," *Review of Educational Research*, 32:179-93, April, 1962.

Stolurow, L. M., "Let's Be Informed on Programmed Instruction," *Phi Delta Kappan*, 44:255-57, March, 1963.

Index